Alabama Blue

Toni K. Pacini

i

Toni K Pacini

DEDICATION

To: Walt (Dockers & tasseled loafers)

Thank you for loving me when I could not love myself.
Believing in me when all I saw was my failures.
Really seeing me – making me visible.
There are no words that can truly thank you for your
amazing love.
You couldn't have told me how great our life could be –
I wouldn't have believed you. I had to see it for myself.

My love always.
Toni (Jeans and moccasins)

ACKNOWLEDGMENTS

I cannot take full credit for Alabama Blue. I would still be sitting on it if it weren't for my unbelievable friends. I was once told that when one dies if she can count on one hand the people who really knew and loved her, she is fortunate indeed. If that is true, I am the most fortunate woman on Earth, because of all of you, and I love you.

The elderly gentleman at the Hatcheck counter, Albany N.Y. 1972 – Who introduced me to reading and a love of the written word. Because of you I discovered that I am important for more than what's between my legs. You made me acutely aware of what's between my ears. I thank you most of all kind Sir.

Walt Bacharowski ~ My partner, my love, my heart.

David Kelley ~ My amazing Brother, I adore you.

Tina Willis ~ Total sunshine, my soul sister and confidant.

Judy Logan ~ Mom of my Heart.

Leslie Hoffman ~ Dear friend and editor extraordinaire.

Amanda Skenendore ~ A kind and gentle guiding light.

Andres Fragoso, Jr. ~ Your encouragement got me off the fence and into the game. Thank you. Alabama Blue, would be only a "script in a drawer," if not for you. I love you.

Peggi Mitchell ~ Thank you for being the first to read my book, my dear friend.

K. B. "Burt" ~ Your friendship gave me worth.

Annette and George ~ In my heart, we are family.

SPECIAL THANKS TO:

Professor Yelena Bailey-Kirby ~ For teaching me that I <u>can</u> learn at sixty!

My Sin City Writer's Group members and friends. What a wonderful group of extremely talented people.

My fellow authors and friends at Henderson Writers' Group for your gentle support, laughter and love.

There are others ~ too many to list here. But I'm a grateful and fortunate woman to know each of you. Thanks for that and so much more.

Love,
Toni

Toni K Pacini

REVIEWS

"Alabama Blue is a memoir that reads like a Southern Gothic novel. Close your eyes. That's right, shut 'em tight. Now, imagine you're six-years-old, peeking around from behind your bedroom door, frightened, shaking, and forcing yourself not to scream while a cab driver collects his fare by violently raping your mother. The same cab driver your momma left you alone with while she went into the liquor store to buy a pint of vodka.

Imprinted into her memory like a tattoo, forty-three years later, Toni Pacini decided it was time to "write the story that lived inside her." That meant leaving her home in California and driving back to Opelika, Alabama to relive her tumultuous youth. Pacini's riveting prose compels the reader to ride shotgun on her journey of self-discovery and self-acceptance. Along the way, you'll cry with her, laugh with her, and cheer for her while she searches for her pot of gold at the end of the rainbow—love."

Leslie E. Hoffman - Author/Editor

"Toni Pacini is a hell of a good writer. Her debut novel, an autobiographical odyssey entitled Alabama Blue, will pull you in and not let you go until the last page is turned. Fortitude, heart, soul...penned in blood and tears, this novel has it all. Expect to be inspired and uplifted, even as you catch your breath from the raw emotions."

Barb Wilson - Author and Editor

Contents

Alabama Blue

Opelika, Alabama

Natural Born Actress — 1960

Momma created chaos and breathed insanity, like a twisted composer creating a maddening tune. The tune might be awful and hard to listen to, but at some level, you respected the composer's ability to create it. Momma wasn't just crazy, she was a carrier. She spread the disorder wherever she went. It was my birth gift. Momma had a way of driving men crazy, too, but not in a good way. I mean out of their minds and out of control insane. Momma would flirt, tease, do and say whatever was necessary to get a man to buy her a bottle, and then she'd dump him.

On this occasion, as on so many others, Momma's grand master plan backfired on her. Earlier in the evening when she called for a cab to take her to the liquor store, she knew she only had enough money for her vodka and not enough to pay for the cab. Clever as always, Momma had the cab-driver pick us up one block over from our house in the mill village. She made me go along 'cause it always looked better to have a kid in tow. The cab driver parked the cab, and he and I waited in the parking lot of the state-run liquor store– they were called package stores back then– with me

1

fidgeting nervously in the back seat while Momma went in to get her medicine.

As soon as my momma was out of sight, he turned so he could hang over the front seat and look me straight in the eyes when he said, "You gonna be a looker like yo' momma. I bet you already got boys sniffin' 'round you like a pack of dogs." I cringed and jerked away when his hairy hand reached out and touched my bare leg, up near the cuff of my shorts. He laughed. When he caught sight of Momma heading our way, he turned back to his steering wheel. I wished I could open the door and run and run, but I knew, even then, there would be nowhere to run to, nowhere to hide.

Once back in the cab, Momma opened her pint of vodka and slid its neck out of the brown paper bag just enough to get her lips around it before we even pulled out of the parking lot. After desperately sucking a gulp, Momma began to talk-up the cab driver. Momma was always goin' on about how she could talk just about anyone into just about anything, given enough time.

When the driver parked on the street where he had originally picked us up, in front of the house he reasonably assumed to be our home, Momma pretended to be ever so surprised to discover that she didn't have enough money in her purse to pay him. She assured him that she had more money in the house, and if he'd sit tight for a minute, she'd be right back. My momma was always an extraordinary actress.

Momma got out of the cab and strolled ever so casually, with my hand in hers, around the side of the house as if she intended to go in the back door. As soon as we were out of his range of vision, she ran. I ran, too, not wanting to be left alone in the neighbor's yard when the cab driver man came looking for us. We ran across the back yards to our house. Momma burst through our door and erupted into laughter at the stupidity of the driver. If she'd been sober, she would have been afraid, but Momma feared nothin' and no one, after a couple of drinks.

My momma, Genell Lois Aldridge, was a natural born actress. She'd honed the art through trial and error over the many years of her ongoing performances. On that particular night though, she ticked off the wrong audience. We had been home for an hour or so when the noise began. Momma had drunk most of her beloved bottle and passed out on the couch, holding her bottle lovingly to her chest. I don't know how he found us, but the cab driver screamed obscenities while he banged his fist against our flimsy front door. I cannot remember if we'd left the door unlocked, or if he kicked it in. I just know that he got in.

I ran into the bedroom as soon as the crazy began, and when he burst through the front door, I scooted under the bed. But I couldn't stay there while he yelled at momma, so I crawled out quiet as a wish on a shooting star. The door was almost closed, but ajar just enough for me to peek through the crack.

There, hidden behind the door, I watched, afraid to see what was going on, yet terrified not to know. He tried to wake Momma, but she was passed out cold. He slapped her and yelled at her. Receiving no response, he went through her purse and pockets. When he found only a few loose coins, he shifted from a simmering rage into full-on crazy and threw the change across the cracked and yellowed linoleum floor. I watched a dime roll on its thin edge, slow down, tremble, and drop. Staring at the dime, I thought about what I could buy with it at the mill store, maybe a moon pie and an RC Cola? My mind ran to that place where I often hid when the alternative was unimaginable.

I tried to look away but couldn't. I saw what he did to my momma. He violently tore the clothes from her limp, defenseless body as I watched from my hiding place, invisible, not making a sound. I wondered why he pulled her legs like that, and I silently screamed for Momma to wake up and stop him. The cab driver pounded his body against Momma so fiercely that it looked like he was beating her with a club. I felt my face contort with horror as I crouched, helpless. Yet, Momma's expression remained flat, emotionless, her head hanging over the edge of the couch, her tongue lolling and spittle sliming from between her silent lips.

Screams welled up in my throat like lava from a once dormant volcano, now desperate for release. I swallowed them as they rose vile and urgent to my lips, before they could betray me. My stomach begged for relief from the swelling emotion, but I kept pushing it down, afraid he might hurt me, too, if he found me hiding there. The next day, Momma was the lucky one. She couldn't remember a thing. Although I was barely six-years-old, I'd remember every horrible detail, forever.

When Memories Assault Us—2003

Forty-three years after the night I watched that dime tremble and drop, I drove back to Alabama from my home in Half Moon Bay, California to visit my brother David. I set out alone one morning, following where my recollections might take me.

When I drove across the old viaduct into Opelika, Alabama and the Golden Cherry Motel came into view, it felt like I'd taken a giant step back in time. The past forty years melted away. I could smell fried chicken, catfish, and hushpuppies. Those familiar scents reminded me of the days when I'd sit at the counter while Momma waited tables in the Golden Cherry's restaurant.

I'd crumble my bacon over the grits and eggs, then mix it all together. I loved it like that, and I'd clean my plate, sopping up the remains with a fat buttermilk biscuit. Sitting there, my short legs dangling from the tall barstool while I waited for Momma to get off work and take me home, I felt so big and special, and, more important, full.

That morning, however, as I drove up and over the viaduct and saw the motel, it felt wrong, like someone had gone and painted the sky brown and the stars pink. When I saw a Domino's Pizza adjoined to the Golden Cherry Motel, my memories started to spin out of control. In fact, they were getting away from me fast, like a balloon that escapes your grasp before it's tied off and goes flitting crazily about the room, then falls deflated to the floor. When what you see contradicts what you remember, it dims the reality of that memory.

With my memory diminished and realizing it would fade more throughout the years to come, I knew only words were left to tell the story. No more Golden Cherry Restaurant, no more counter.

No more dangling legs from tall barstools while eating my eggs and grits. It was all past now, except for the places captured in the 1979 award winning film Norma Rae, starring Sally Field, that was filmed in the mill village where my grandparents, my momma, and so many nameless others worked, lived, and died.

I knew then, at that very moment, that *the book* must be written. The book lived inside me, it's words pushed and nudged at my heart every day and threatened to fall off my tongue at inappropriate times, and sometimes did.

I drove on past the Golden Cherry and turned onto Third Street into the village, where I stopped for a moment in front of the little house that knows my secrets. Driving on through the village and down to the mill, I parked and made a promise to all the invisible little girls who walk the streets, heads down in shame, crippled by blame. I will tell the tale, I will write the book. I will release the words that we all choke on when memories assault us.

Chapter Two - Swallowing the Soap

Cotton Fields to Ocean Blue-1968

The airplane descended delivering me to a world so unbelievably new that I wondered if we might have landed on some distant planet instead of San Francisco, California. As I cautiously exited the belly of my first airplane, I felt as if the huge amazing machine had just birthed me anew. This place was nothing like the place I left just hours before. I felt conspicuous, awkward as if everyone knew that I had just arrived and did not really belong here, that I did not *belong* anywhere.

Half an hour later, I hugged the door of the old truck as the frame rattled and jiggled. My first concern should have been the condition of the vehicle I found myself in. Instead I had less fear of falling out onto the roadway than of the man driving. We were heading south out of San Francisco on Highway 1. My cheek felt cold from where my face pressed against the dingy glass, my breath created a steamy film on the truck window and hindered my view of the endless freeways. There were too many cars, concrete overpasses, and unfamiliar exits leading to mysterious places.

When I came off the plane, dressed in the powder blue pantsuit my grandma bought me the day before from J.C. Penney's and saw him standing there at the gate, I knew he was my daddy, although even more handsome than the two age-yellowed and dog-eared photographs I had known him by until that moment. Momma said my daddy looked like Vince Edwards, the lead actor in the television show, *Ben Casey MD*, that had been popular in the sixties. So every time I saw Vince Edwards on TV, I'd fantasize that he was my daddy. Momma always said, "Your daddy may be a son-of-a-bitch, but he is still one tall, dark, and handsome man." The stranger sitting next to me had thick and wavy black hair. His dark brown eyes seemed to have a light behind them, an energy that drew me to him. Years later I'd come to understand that there is warmth in my daddy's eyes, that's seldom reflected in his manner.

We dropped down a steep hill into the small beachside town of Pacifica. I sat in awe, a fourteen-year-old Alabama girl, completely captivated by my first ocean view. The meandering shoreline, waves of green and blue rushed out toward the horizon and back again to the shore. Swooping, screaming birds diving for their dinner. Rolling green hills speckled with orange poppies waved in bright sunlight. Wildflowers, children, and dogs of all sorts, ships and sailboats, surfers, lovers walking hand in hand, and specks of light dancing on the watery waves like diamonds from Atlantis. Until that day, California and its ocean had been a million miles away in a place where little girls like me were never likely to go. Yet there I was, so unbelievable. I wanted to share my delight with someone, but my daddy hadn't said more than a handful of words since picking me up at the airport.

When I wobbled off the plane, dazed by so much new, so much everything, and saw my daddy standing there, for a moment I thought I was face to face with Vince Edwards. My mind said, "No, he's not an actor, he's your daddy girl." My daddy, I thought, how weird. I ain't never had me no real daddy. I had no idea how I should act, or what I might say? I wanted to run to him, and at the same time I fought the impulse to bolt the other way. My stomach and my eyes threatened to betray me. Grandma had spent money she didn't have on my new clothes so I'd make a good impression. I did not feel impressive. I felt terrified, awkward, and ugly, anything but impressive.

It had been twelve years since Daddy put me on a train with my momma and big sister and sent us back to Alabama. I thought he'd have something to say to me by now, but he did not speak. As the silence hung between us, my terror grew. Why didn't he say something?

For twelve years I had survived the craziness my daddy had sentenced me to when he sent me back to the mill village with my momma, a woman so damaged by life that she never found a moments peace. I created a fantasy throughout the years that my daddy loved and missed me. I needed to believe that my daddy would come for me. I blamed Momma that he never visited, called or wrote.

Finally, at the airport, the stranger before me, my daddy, found his voice and asked if I had any luggage to claim. I held up my little carry on bag and said, "All I got is this here."

He replied, "Then come on."

My daddy turned and walked away. He stood well over six feet tall, so I had to run to keep up with him. The airport was huge, and I thought there were more people in that one place than in all of Alabama put together. Terrified at the thought of being left behind, alone in that new and frightening world, I scurried after the stranger, my parent, like a cowered wolf pup his first time out of the den.

Now in Daddy's work truck, silent as a feather afloat, I remembered an episode of Ben Casey. The story of a little girl who had been terribly abused and would not speak to anyone, she had not spoken one word for months. In a playground scene at the hospital, she sat alone on a still swing, her sorrow hanging from her tiny body like a yoke on an old, tired mare. Ben Casey went out to comfort her, and because of his gentle kindness she surprised him by reciting the following poem for him.

Tiny Tim
I had a little Teddy Bear— his name was Tiny Tim.
I put him in the bathtub to teach him how to swim.
First he ate the bath cloth and then he ate the soap,
I called for the doctor but he said there was no hope.
He died last night with a bubble in his throat.

That little girl's poem gave me words for what I could not say. There was no hope. But why speak of hopelessness? What would that accomplish. It was too late, she and I had already swallowed the soap.

Most adults I had known until that day in San Francisco had considered children to be a nuisance and a bother. I had hoped my daddy would be different. But I saw his discomfort and thinly veiled anger and tasted his frustration. He could barely stand to look at me. When he did, his eyes shifted from one place to another like a trapped animal seeking the nearest exit. Clearly my visit was an unexpected intrusion and not the joyous reunion I had dreamed of.

I accepted the truth, bouncing on the worn bench seat and gripping the door handle until my knuckles turned white, that the caring daddy who missed me, the one who would one day come to rescue me, did not exist.

Though I'd spent years yearning for him, waiting for him, believing in him, it took less than an hour for me to realize that my daddy wanted me to be quiet, invisible, and stay out of his way. I had just traveled 2,700 miles to assume the same role I'd had the day before. Once again, I had swallowed the soap.

Chapter Three - Family Tree

Daddy

A first-generation American, born in San Francisco in December 1930, my daddy started his life on more solid ground than his father had. At twenty years old Grandpa Ruggerio boarded a boat in Italy headed for America. He was ecstatic when he arrived at Ellis Island under the watchful eye of the Statue of Liberty, awed by her beauty and grace.

He stood in the long lines being processed through immigration, weary from travel, yet energized by hope. Papers were checked and facts documented, eventually the authorities allowed Grandpa Ruggerio to enter America.

Following written directions given to him by a family member who had already made the journey, he boarded a train bound for California and his new life. Once settled in his seat, his small bag filled with all he possessed stowed carefully under his legs for safekeeping, he took the first deep breath he'd had since he left his homeland. The trip had been exhausting and often frightening, at times he had feared he'd never see America. Knowing his papers were accepted and being safely seated aboard a train bound for his new home, he felt safe for the first time in far too long.

Soon after his arrival in Fresno, California, Ruggerio married a pig farmer's daughter named Emilia. Emilia and her family were immigrants from Italy as well. In her early to mid-teens, she was too young to be a wife and too old to be a child. In line with the norm in a good Italian Catholic family, in less than a year Emilia found herself swollen with child and stayed that way for the next several years, having four babies by the time she turned twenty.

Emilia ran away two years after the birth of her last child, my daddy Carlo. Women did not abandon their children in those days, no matter what, so Emilia's leaving sent a clear message to my daddy that he mattered little to anyone.

After Emilia's disappearance, her children were scattered. My daddy, the only one of Emilia's children who stayed with my grandfather, was cared for by first one family member and then another for the next few years. When Daddy was four years old Grandpa left him at a shelter for children in San Mateo, California.

Ruggerio, who had come to be known by the more American name Roger, reclaimed my daddy when he was twelve. He intended to bring all of his son's back together to work on his ranch in San Gregorio south of San Francisco. None of the others returned – they were older and had other options.

Daddy went home with Roger that day, but his father's house would never be my daddy's *home*. His stepmother only allowed him in the house to sleep and he ate his meals alone on the porch. More often than not he had to buy his own food. He went to school in Santa Cruz and worked a variety of odd jobs.

In 1951 Daddy joined the Army, stationed at Ft. Benning Army base in Georgia where he served as a Sergeant in the Paratroopers. This is how he ended up in Opelika, Alabama, on a chilly December evening in 1951, and how he became the third husband of Genell Lois Aldridge, a mill village girl.

Momma

Born on April 8, 1926. Irish, Native American, and French, Momma inherited all the best features of her ancestors. With thick and wavy dark hair, high cheekbones, stunning hazel eyes, and a trim, shapely figure, she turned all the men's heads. An extravert that people warmed to easily, attractive, outgoing, and talented, but Momma was a terribly damaged woman. One of those people that other people would comment about:

"What a shame, she had such potential."

She loved to sing and even sang backup once for Hank Williams at WJHO Radio in Opelika. Musicians at the time didn't have the luxury of television exposure and music videos to advertise their albums. So they traveled around the country doing live shows, performing mostly at juke joints, which were Momma's kind of scene, and they would sing live on local radio stations to promote their next gig.

Momma had an impressive voice, so it was no surprise to the locals when WJHO recommended her to Hank Williams. The country music star asked Momma to sing backup for him live on the air during his radio broadcast, a memory she cherished.

She also wrote beautiful poetry, though limited by her lack of education, her poems were intelligent and passionate. She drew simple expressive drawings, played the spoons and a little slide guitar, using a butter knife as a slide. Throughout the years she won several jitterbug dance contests.

My Momma was one of a kind, an especially rare woman for the time and place she occupied. Unfortunately, she was one of the walking wounded, another one who hadn't survived her childhood unscathed. The only peace she ever found was in a vodka bottle.

Just Another Mill Village Girl

Momma married twice before marrying my daddy in 1951, always in the same futile attempt to escape the unbelievable nightmare that was her life. Born in Tallassee, Alabama, where her parents met and married. Momma's parents worked long hard hours in the cotton mill and her father had a fiery, slightly psychotic temper and a drinking problem.

Grandpa had butted heads with the management in the mill for some time. When they threatened to reduce his hours, pride got the better of him and he quit right there, not just for himself but for his wife as well. With no options or jobs available in Tallassee,

Grandpa moved his young family into Pepperell Mill Village in Opelika, Alabama, where he and Grandma went to work in the West Point Pepperell Cotton Mill.

The village was composed of rows of simple little white four-room homes. The textile industries built these villages across the south to take advantage of the poor, illiterate, lower white class. Most poor white families of that time did not own a car and often lived outside the city limits, making it difficult to get to work at the mills.

The company village offered families cheap housing, an elementary school, a company store, a company nurse, and a post office. This is the ultimate example of the phrase, "He owed his soul to the company store." Once a family moved there and became enmeshed in the system, they seldom left. Generation after generation would work and die in these little mill-generated worlds.

Momma's Missed Childhood

Momma's parents made her quit school in the fourth grade and stay home to take care of her brothers. A child herself, small, confused and uneducated, Momma reluctantly assumed the roles of parent and housekeeper. Of all the things taken from her throughout the years, I think she missed her childhood the most.

The drinking started about this time. With both parents working late shift and sleeping during the day, Momma had every opportunity to party. She became quite good at deception, although it's easy to deceive when no one is paying attention.

Several evenings each week, as soon as Grandma and Grandpa were out of sight, Momma's friends would start showing up. One would have a few cigarettes he had pinched from his daddy and another, a beer or two. Soon there would be a game of cards or spin the bottle, and for a while Momma would be the belle of the ball, the center of attention she so desperately needed. Although it was not the same as a scene from the school playground, complete with pretty hair ribbons and silly little boys making stupid faces, trying to get the girl's attention, sadly this was the only life she had.

As soon as she was even close to old enough, she began running away and later getting married. Momma would marry seven times in her short life. Marriage was the only escape for a dirt-poor, uneducated, mill village girl.

The Party Begins

In the Army, stationed at Fort Benning in Georgia, my daddy stood in the doorway of the gloomy gray barracks on December 28, 1951, his birthday. He wanted to celebrate, but he had no friends or family in the South. Eventually loneliness won out over his dread of the cold, dark winter day, and he set out hitchhiking. He had no plan and eventually he stumbled into the small town of Opelika, Alabama. As he stepped from the empty street into a dingy little restaurant, his gaze fell on a willowy, dark-haired beauty with dancing eyes and a ready smile. She warmed him with her wit and easy manner. Their meeting was the beginning of one hell of a party.

My momma loved to dance, Daddy loved to gamble, and they both loved to drink. The Army Base and downtown Columbus had multiple nightclubs filled with music, booze, and gambling halls. My parents were sure that life had finally dealt two drifting, lonely souls a winning hand. Together their lives would be about more than just survival. They were young and in love, and life looked promising.

They married in a leap year on February 29, 1952. My sister, Deborah Bathsheba, was born almost exactly one year later. The arrival of their first child should have been a time of celebration. Instead it helped to escalate events that would eventually destroy their marriage. A normal newborn, Deborah needed constant attention, love, and care. Unfortunately, our momma did not have the ability to care for an infant, and Deborah would always be labeled a difficult baby.

Deborah cried nonstop for the first two-and-a-half years of her life. I'm sure my sister was only asking to be seen, heard, and loved, but although the band had stopped playing, Momma couldn't stop the dance. Momma had been drinking since her early teens and qualified as a full-blown alcoholic by the time she met my daddy. She often joked throughout the years, almost like a boast, that when she gave birth to Deborah, her water didn't break, her vodka did.

Grandma 1906-1976

A stunning woman, tall and dignified with beautiful skin. I remember admiring my grandmother as she moisturized daily with Jergen's lotion. I'd marvel at her gentle and graceful manner as she slathered the cool lotion over her pale white skin in a slow, almost sensual manner. I am looking at Grandma now as I write this. I keep a black and white photograph of her on my computer. She is wearing a black dress with a strand of pearls around her slender neck.

Grandma had those pearls for as long as my memory serves, and wore them almost every time she had an occasion to dress up. Like so many things in life, they looked good from a distance, however upon closer inspection you could see where the white finish had worn off the cheap beads in several places. I remember how the beads felt between my fingers and how I had to fight the temptation to pick at and pull off the flaking paint.

Beside Grandma's photograph is a note I typed years ago; "Grandma, I tell the tales you could not tell." I am not sure she'd approve. Our lives were a lot like Grandma's pearls. From a distance, they looked okay. With my words, I am slowly peeling off the false surface of our lives and revealing the truth hidden beneath.

Never Measure Up

One morning I awoke alone in the bedroom I shared with my sister, momma, and sometimes with my Uncle Jimmy on one of the many occasions that he'd be between wives, jobs, or drunks. We occupied a small room, sparsely decorated with a full and a twin bed, and just enough room between the two for a small night table. At the foot of the larger bed, a chest of drawers sat wedged in the corner. With so many people under one roof, one rarely had a moment alone. Yet when I awoke, I found no one in the little room with me.

What a beautiful day, the sun streaming in the open-screened windows. A slight breeze fluttered the light drapes. To be alone in the room, any room, made me feel special. I got up and made the bed. Maybe five years old and small, I had to stand on the tips of my toes to pull the covers up and then I'd crawl onto the bed to cover the middle. This was no easy task since we had a boxed spring and at least two mattresses on each bed. My grandparents did this because in the wintertime, when the heat from the wood, coal, or gas heater would rise to the ceiling, you'd be warmer up high.

Some people had little steps built for the children – we just crawled up and slid down. So I crawled up and pulled and tugged until convinced the bed looked real pretty, then I slid down to the floor and started straightening the sides. I imagined how pleased Grandma would be when she saw what a great job I had done. Before I could finish my surprise for her, she came into the room screaming, "What the devil are you doing in here, child? Look at that mess you're making. You can't make no bed. Git out of here. Go on I said, git now and let me make this bed proper."

I slithered away, once again reminded that I should be invisible and stay out of the way. Grandma always made it clear that no one was capable of doing anything right except her. Everything had to be just so. She needed to believe no one could do things better than her; if you proved her wrong, you took away her purpose, her reason for existing. At least she had one.

Grandpa, 1904-1974

A heavy drinker in the days before the cancer, Grandpa Aldridge smoked, drank, and raised hell. Most of the hell he raised he directed toward his family. This created secrets that my grandparents insisted never be shared outside of our home.

"Don't let the neighbors know. Never tell."

A big part of Grandma's purpose was cleaning up after Grandpa's tirades so no one would know what went on inside our thin walls. Frequently Grandma would take a long, cane pole, designed especially for this purpose with a scoop on the end, and fish Grandpa's teeth out of the outhouse hole after he lost his dentures, along with his cookies, the night before. Grandma's father was a raging drunk too; maybe that is why she seemed to accept such duties as simply part of being a wife.

Grandpa had been adopted, and I never heard much of his history. His birth name was Oliver Sullivan Aldridge. He professed to be Irish and he looked Irish, but his surname, Aldridge, is a Sax name. The majority of Aldridge's I researched came from Wales, another mystery.

Throughout my childhood, no one talked about race. Anyone who wasn't a pure white Protestant must be a heathen sinner or a foreigner to be watched. Of course, most of those pure white Protestants were at least part Native American, who were called Indians in those days, or African American – I won't say what they were called, or Polish, Greek, Italian, or – fill in the blank –

23

Americans. However, no one would admit their true blood, their heritage, because of well-placed fears of discrimination.

The last names and faces told the story, yet no one spoke the truth. Working in the mill and living in the village automatically labeled us as white trash. So the dirty laundry and our personal roots stayed buried in shame at the bottom of an invisible, well-guarded closet. So much so that my siblings and I grew up not really being sure of our own true heritage and nationality.

What a sad society that makes one's roots a source of shame. Our lives were built on generation after generation of shame. How the "telling" heals. That's why I sit at my keyboard tonight, the eve of Thanksgiving, alone, lost in the telling. Grandma couldn't tell; she just kept cleaning. Momma could never tell. She just kept drinking.

Snake-eyes

I can still smell him, a combination of Old Spice mixed with the pungent aroma of chewing tobacco. Grandpa took a bath every Saturday, whether he needed it or not, and he always made a major production of it. He had a way of dramatizing everything, and after a performance or the telling of a tale, he always concluded by saying, "*Snake-eyes*." No one knows why.

He quit drinking alcohol and smoking cigarettes on July 26, 1950, the day the doctors removed one of his lungs due to cancer. That same day grandma gladly retired her cane pole, no longer needing to rescue grandpa's dentures from the outhouse. Absent the

24

booze, it soon became clear to everyone, except Grandpa, that he had been self-medicating a serious mental problem. Years later, after bizarre episodes where he'd accuse my grandmother of having affairs with the mailman and the paperboy, the doctor's diagnosed Grandpa a paranoid schizophrenic.

After Grandpa's lung was removed, he spent the rest of his life dying. I cannot remember the passing of any holiday or anyone's birthday that he did not announce with sincere reverence, "I ain't gonna be here this time next year."

Yet he lived for almost twenty-five years after his surgery. I can still see him sitting in his chair, his pocketknife – which had a bone overlay handle, yellowed by age – in one hand and a square of Red Bull tobacco in the other. He'd cut off a plug and plop it into his mouth, never far from the sweet pea can he used as a portable spittoon. His face was very wrinkled, and the tobacco juice would collect in tiny rivulets at the corners of his mouth.

Grandpa always had a pocketful of toilet paper, and to pass the time, he'd entertain himself as well as us kids by rolling tiny squares of paper like mini tusks and horns and stick them in his ears, nose, and mouth, a poor man's origami. Once when a young girl from the village was visiting me, Grandpa couldn't help himself – he loved a new audience and so he had paper sticking out all over. Angie already found this as odd as I found it embarrassing, then for his grand finale, Grandpa stuck out his tobacco juice-covered dentures and little Angie ran home in terror and would never come into our house again. Grandpa roared with laughter; he found his antics hilarious. I did not.

Almost daily he'd walk the quarter mile down the highway to Dubois' Service Station. Since the removal of his lung, grandpa walked bent and hunchbacked. He appeared to be walking against a harsh wind. He'd sit with his friends on a bench in front of the station for hours. The ground around the old men's feet and the tops of their shoes would be covered with tiny wood shavings. Some pieces were blonde or almost white; others a variety of reds and browns. Whittling small pieces of wood with their pocketknives kept their hands busy and gave them an excuse not to look at each other as they talked.

Grandpa sat there all morning till he had to get home for lunch or risk catching hell from Grandma. He spent hours gossiping with the other men who were too sick or old to go into the mill anymore. They heatedly debated politics, religion, and anything else that came up. Momma called that bench, "The dead peter bench." Now that's funny.

The Ceiling Fairy

One of my few fond memories of Grandpa was when he'd have me sit on his lap while he told me the story of the fairy that lived in a little hole in the corner of our living room ceiling. He told me to look at the hole and concentrate really, really hard, and I might get to see her. I would. I'd concentrate so hard while watching for the arrival of the fairy, so focused on that little hole in the ceiling, that when all of a sudden candy would fall from the heavens I'd jump, startled from my concentration. I'd slide off Grandpa's lap and run around the small room gathering my special presents from the fairy. When I got old enough, I caught Grandpa tossing the candies with his right hand, while distracting me with his left.

Grandpa's only household responsibility was washing the dinner dishes. He'd ceremoniously put on the long, white apron that fell below his knees and filled the two speckled and chipped enamel bowls in the sink, one to wash the dishes and one to rinse. If in a good mood, he'd sing, when he wasn't talking to himself. Grandpa often made up his own silly little ditties, a habit I inherited. But he did not make up his favorite song "Adam and Eve in the Garden," although I have never heard it anywhere except from his lips.

It went like this:

Adam and Eve in the garden when the world was very new.
The earth just contained two, and dressmakers very few.
Now Adam said to Eve in the garden,
I have a dandy scheme for you.
When autumn comes I'll tell you what we'll do.
You'll wear a tulip, a big yellow tulip,
and I'll wear a big red rose.
And in Adam's expressing, you could tell by assessing.

That he had invented clothes.

Now all the girls in the city were all very pretty,

They each had a smile that glowed.

But if the styles keep on daring all the girls will be

wearing - is a smile and a great big rose.

And as always, Grandpa concluded his performance

with, "Snake-eyes!"

Chapter Four – Twisted Branches - Broken Tree

Family Secrets

We always traveled on a clear day in spring or summer because Grandpa wouldn't drive any further than Piggly Wiggly in winter or during bad weather. If the sky were clear and the right time of year, we'd all load up in Old Betsy and head off to visit some relative or the other. Grandpa called every car he ever owned "Old Betsy," and he'd talk to her up and down the road like she really understood him. He'd pat the dashboard or the steering wheel with affectionate encouragement as you might do with a stubborn horse balking at crossing a stream, and say, "Come on Old Betsy, be a good ole girl; there ya go, that's my girl."

Grandma would pack bologna, deviled ham, or pimento cheese sandwiches on white bread and wrap them in waxed paper. Sometimes we'd have potato salad and fried chicken and her "special fixin's," my favorite being deviled eggs. We would stop somewhere along the way on the side of the road to eat, pee, and rest.

An awful driver, while behind the wheel Grandpa would be tense and eager to blame others if he made an error. His passengers sat rigid and silent, clinging to the door handles, afraid to speak or even cough. He drove so slowly that we could watch a bug crawl up a fence post as we passed it.

There were no freeways, just old, rutted highways and back roads lined with dust-covered trees and endless miles of kudzu. The towns we drove through were usually no more than a water tower, a stretch of railroad track, and a church.

These tiny towns awakened us from our road-trip induced trances and prompted us to sit up straight and stare, unwilling to risk missing anything that might be interesting. Each new zip code or county that we creeped through at a snail's pace, looked old and poor, and tired to the bone. In those days' no one had air-conditioners in their homes, and certainly not in their automobiles. So on these little trips we had no choice other than to keep the windows rolled down and inhale the exhaust along with the bugs. By the time we reached our destination we'd all be irritable, hot, sticky, exhausted, and covered with a fine layer of red road dust.

In the spring of 1961, I found myself wedged in between my momma and Uncle Jimmy in the backseat of Old Betsy, going to visit relatives in Tallassee, which in itself wasn't so bad, but I dreaded seeing Uncle Frank, my Grandpa's older brother. Whenever we went to see him or he visited us, he and Grandpa would sit on the front porch and argue at the top of their lungs – in Grandpa's case, lung – about their views of God and their personal and often disturbing interpretations of the Bible.

A Baptist preacher, Uncle Frank considered himself divinely appointed. His conversations were always riddled with endless references to Hell, the righteous wrath of God, divine punishment, damnation, Satan, demons, and other fear based gibberish. Momma hated Uncle Frank, and she made little effort to be civil, only enough so to keep Grandma and Grandpa off her back. My sister and I instinctively tried to avoid Uncle Frank. We couldn't understand or explain our feelings when we were young, but he always felt "yucky" and frightened us.

Just after my ninth birthday I overheard a conversation that explained a lot. Apparently the Baptist church had defrocked Uncle Frank many years before when a parishioner caught him raping a black woman in the church. He had hired her to clean and once he had her powerless and alone in the church, a place that should depict safety, he brutally raped her. Of course, no legal action was taken. In that time and place, a woman would have no justice in such a matter, especially a black woman. Charges would sooner have been brought against Uncle Frank if he had raped Billy Joe Bob's prize winning huntin' dog.

Although defrocked, Uncle Frank continued to call himself Reverend Aldridge until the day he died. Many years later, with the assistance of extensive therapy, I began to piece together the bits of information in my scattered mind files and understand Momma's intense hatred for Uncle Frank.

In hindsight I can see clearly the classic incest survivor traits that permeated my mother's life: anorexia, depression, self-abuse, and a deep-seeded distrust and disgust for men as a whole. Years ago, Yoko Ono sang and recorded a song written by John Lennon, "Woman is the Nigger of the world." She got that right.

Branches

My grandmother was named Olemenell Hughey, but everyone called her Nell. She had four sisters and one brother: Clementine, Kate, Irene, Tiny, and Fred. I never knew Aunt Tiny's real name. She stood five–foot and two–inches tall and topped three hundred pounds, so I couldn't understand why people called her Tiny. Just one more example of that good old Southern kindness I often heard about and seldom saw.

I only recall one visit to Tiny's house. I have a vivid, almost surreal memory of her little dilapidated home, no more than a four-room shack with an outhouse, one with a crescent moon carved into the door. She had a milk cow, chickens, and a little garden with all sorts of good things.

When we arrived we found her sitting outside in the shade on a circular wooden bench, built around a stout old oak tree. She had her short round legs spread wide under her hiked-up skirt in a not-so-modest attempt to cool herself in the suffocating summer heat. Her legs looked like huge, overstuffed sausages, the rolls of fat mottled with a red heat rash. We sat a while as she snapped peas and shucked corn for our dinner. Later, once it cooled down a bit, I became mesmerized watching her churn butter as she perched precariously spread legged on the edge of a chair, working a pole up and down in an old wooden barrel.

Aunt Tiny shared my grandmother's obsession with cleanliness. It must have been a part of the Hughey girls' DNA. Aunt Tiny swept her yard every day with a house broom, not a rake; she kept it as smooth as a floor. Any sticks or rocks you saw were stacked in neat little piles or used to border the flowerbeds or trees.

I didn't like Aunt Tiny much. She seemed to see children the same way she saw yard dogs. I got the clear, yet unspoken message from her to "shut up and stay out from underfoot, and you might get a scrap or two." Eccentricity was a trait found on every twisted branch of our family tree. Some branches were more gnarled than others were.

Out On a Limb

In 1956, Daddy, finally fed up with momma's drunkenness and downright meanness, physical abuse, temper tantrums, and her constant whining about being homesick for Alabama, sent Momma, my sister Deborah and me back to Alabama on a train. We moved in with my grandparents in the cotton mill village, where we remained for two and a half years. Until my mid-forties, that two plus years at my grandparents would be the longest time I ever lived in one place, having moved in excess of fifty times before my sixteenth birthday.

I have little memory of those years, but most of the photographs that were ever taken of my sister and me had been taken in April of 1958. The developer stamped the date on each picture, not knowing at the time that he'd later provide me with the only solid evidence of my childhood.

In some of the photographs we are posed in cute shorts outfits or matching pajamas. There are a few of us in bed pretending to sleep or on our knees pretending to pray. In others we are shown holding a rifle or a fishing pole, and there are even a few of us nude and holding cigarettes. Yeah, that's weird, even odder is the fact that those photographs depict a childhood we never had.

They were all posed. The clothes and props must have been bought or borrowed especially for the pictures, the rifle, fishing pole, toy guitar, sombrero, and cigarettes. The scenes simply did not fit our reality. The shots of us pretending to pray and sleep weren't even taken in our bedroom. They were taken in our grandparents' bedroom where we were not allowed.

Long after Daddy sent us back to Alabama, Momma held on to the belief that he'd miss her and send for us. He had no intention of doing so. She panicked when he filed for a divorce, but she still thought she could convince him to take her back. She wrote long letters, begging him to reconsider, but they went unanswered. When notified by mail in March of 1958 that the divorce would be final as of the third of February, she fell apart and that's when all the pictures of Deborah and me were taken.

The photographs had been Momma's last desperate attempt to get my daddy to take us back. If he wouldn't reconcile for her, maybe he'd do it for us. She sent the photographs off, along with her last shreds of hope and pride, and awaited the miracle that would surely come. There would be no answer, no one-way tickets and no reconciliation. She finally had to accept, once again, that there would be no escape. Momma's escapes had been largely imaginary and always temporary.

The saddest thing about the photos taken in 1958 is that they were the only really good pictures ever taken of us. Throughout the following years there were no photos of Christmas by the tree, no birthday parties, no Halloween costumes, no pony rides, no pictures of us swimming or riding a bike, no first day of school, no science projects, no childhood. Most of the above scenes never happened or had been shabby at best. Whatever did happen would be lost in the chaos, and we have no proof that any of it ever occurred at all.

From left to right: Toni, Deborah

The Salesman - 1959

Momma finally gave up the last bit of hope she had that someday, somehow, my daddy would take her back and she moved on. I had just turned five when she married husband number four. In what appeared to be a system she used for finding mates, Momma took a waitress job in Opelika and soon met Mike Kerns, a traveling salesman of some sort, from Detroit, Michigan. The restaurant sat at the entrance to the only movie theatre in town. My sister Deborah and I seldom got to go the movies, but Mike would treat us to a show so he could be alone with momma.

Mike would purchase our tickets at the booth and he and Momma would send me along, accompanied by my big sister, into the darkness of the long walkway that led into the concession area. Sometimes Mike or Momma would even give us money for popcorn and a Coke. The theatre only had one screen so you had no choice of movies.

That's where I saw the movie *The Fly,* which terrified me. I begged to go home, but we were not allowed to leave the theatre until the movie ended and Momma and Mike came for us. I had nightmares about *The Fly* for years. I didn't need more fuel to stoke my fear. At five I could not go to sleep by myself in a dark room because the grownups used terror, real or fictional, to control children. There were demons in the wall sockets; ghosts on the back porch and the burners on top of the gas stove had been called eyes because they were the eyes of a monster. My all-time favorite from the seemingly endless list of horrors was snakes under the bed.

"Do not get out of bed alone, or the snakes will wrap around your legs and pull you under into their world."

If I awoke in the night and had to go to the toilet, I'd have to call out for someone to come in and turn on the light so the snakes wouldn't get me. My sister resented me because she would have to go to bed with me when I woke terrified, so she added to my terror by telling me scary stories that a five-year-old should never hear and a six-year-old should not know.

I'd beg her to stop and cover my ears with my hands while trilling, "La-La-La-La-La." I still heard her. Up until my late twenties, if I woke in the night and found my foot or hand hanging over the edge of the bed, I'd snatch it back in horror. Although old enough to know there were no snakes under my bed, my heart would still pound for several minutes there alone in the night with no one to turn on the light for me. Terror is an excellent way to keep children in bed, but I don't recommend it.

One-Way Tickets

At thirty-two years old Momma married Mike, the salesman from Detroit. They had known each other for less than a month when they tied the knot in my grandparents' living room. After the brief ceremony, they packed us up and we headed off to Detroit in Mike Kern's old car. Mike boasted about a beautiful home and promised a happy-ever-after. As it turned out, he did have a nice brick home, but what a god-awful mess.

A widower, Mike had four children from three to eight years old. I don't know who Mike had stay with his children while he ran off being a traveling salesman and getting married, but they must have just tossed food in the door and ran. The house was filthy and the children were wild and hungry. The youngest one, who ran around naked most of the time, would take his food behind the couch to eat, and he relieved himself wherever he happened to be when the urge came over him. My sister and I had seen filth and chaos before and would see a lot more in the years that followed, however never like we saw at Mike' house.

Momma shoveled the place out and got it into better order. After a few weeks Mike left on a sales trip and the games began. He left money for food, which Momma spent mostly on booze and cigarettes. Tiny hands quickly hoarded away the little food she did buy. Our new family only had one thing in common, the nightmare we all shared.

A week or maybe two passed, and finally Mike returned from his trip to find the home front worse than ever, well, at least just as bad as before we moved in. He didn't burn any daylight getting us to the bus station. He handed Momma our one-way tickets back to Alabama and we boarded that old Greyhound dog. Seems like Momma's husbands sent us on a lot of one-way trips.

Chapter Five - Momma's Battered Bough

I'm Talking Now

Momma chain-smoked and I had bronchial asthma, never a good combination. She did this weird thing with her cigarettes where she'd extract the filter with her front teeth – which made her look like a little gopher – in the process fibers from the filter would get in her mouth and she'd spit. Momma's clothing, bedding, and most of our household furnishings were covered with loose bits of tobacco and tiny burn holes, and she left a trail of filters and butts wherever she went.

When I had an asthma attack, I'd beg Momma not to smoke, but my asking her to put out a cigarette would only infuriate her and she'd yell at me, "Don't be so stupid. You'd have to smoke the damned cigarette yourself for it to hurt you. Hush up and leave me alone, I ain't got no mind to be bossed around by no damned young'un."

So I'd shut up and concentrate on each labored breath, hoping the next one *would* come. At times I honestly thought my lungs would explode. I couldn't hold my breath but I learned well to hold my tongue. I spent the most part of my childhood being quiet and staying out of the way, attempting to dissolve into each moment to the point of transparency.

Things were bad when we lived with my grandparents, even worse when momma moved us into our own place, especially if we moved outside of the mill village away from grandma and grandpa. Alone with Momma, Deborah and I could do pretty much whatever we pleased, which is not a good thing, children need supervision. Those days were terrifying.

Every few months Momma would get a job as a waitress or store clerk, or go back to work in the mill. Then Momma would move us into some choice rat hole. Most of the places that momma rented weren't places other people would consider occupying. So, she'd usually make a deal with some desperate slumlord to pay her first week or month's rent when she got her first check from her new job.

Momma would be all excited, full of promises that never came to be, and off we'd go…again. She rarely lasted more than a month before she got drunk and lost her job. Some of her drunks could last for weeks, and in the meanwhile, the laundry would pile up, food would run out, the electricity would be turned off, and the landlords, truant officers, and, eventually, my grandparents would start banging on the door.

At that point my sister and I would be prisoners in the house. We were afraid to open a curtain or take a step outside. If Momma got busted, she'd blame us. We hid like trapped frightened animals in the darkness, eating whatever we could find. The place would soon smell awful and in the winter months if the electricity had been

40

turned off because momma drank the utility money, we froze. In the summer time, we cooked in the unbearable Southern heat since we had to keep the windows and doors closed and bolted against the threat of discovery.

In my mid-thirties a doctor diagnosed me with Post-Traumatic Stress Disorder, which explains why the smell of mold, puke, and urine occasionally triggers such fear and sorrow for me. How odd the things our bodies, especially the nose, will remember.

When on a drunk, Momma's greatest fear was that her parents would catch her drinking. Not only because all hell would rain down on her, but also once her parents showed up she knew that the party would be over. When my sister and I were old enough to do so, we would sometimes ask a neighbor to call our grandparents to come rescue us. Momma would punish us for that the rest of her life. Now, we were the enemy, too.

Whenever my grandparents did show up they created a scene in the process. They'd come through the door screaming, shaming, and blaming. Grandma always did most of the talking: "Look at this filthy place, Genell. What in the name of God is wrong with you? How can you live like this?"

On most occasions, Momma would be passed out or at least beyond the point of logical response. Grandma would scream at her, "Answer me, damn you, answer me!"

Momma would mumble some drunken response or obscenity, to which Grandma would inevitably respond, "Shut up, you shut your vulgar mouth or I'll kill you."

These conversations, screaming matches, had been so confusing,

"Answer me! Shut up!"

Most of my childhood was nonsensical.

I'd tell Grandma, "I'm sorry grandma, please don't be mad, I'm sorry."

I always apologized to Momma, for Momma, and to everyone else. Momma had raised me well to accept this burden of guilt. From as early as my first memory, I remember Momma telling me that if only I had died in her womb my daddy would not have left her, she wouldn't be poor and lonely, and therefore she would not get drunk.

Momma shared in great detail how she had tried to end my life by jabbing cold metal clothes hangers into herself in a desperate attempt to rip me from my warm, quiet nest. She described the pain of her self-abuse. The bitter taste of the household poisons she drank, how she'd throw up until she could no longer stand then slide wearily down onto the linoleum, holding onto the fowl smelling toilet, weak from sorrow and the chore of trying to kill her own flesh and blood.

She reminisced about jumping off of a high porch and then running back up the steps to do it again and again. I heard her pain and felt her heavy regret until I truly was sorry that I had not died in her womb, as she desired. Saying "I'm sorry" only fueled my grandparents' rage.

"I'm sorry, Grandma."

She'd agree with me. "You sure are sorry. The whole lot of you ain't nothin' but sorry worthless trash."

There was no real dialogue. Early on I learned to hold my words. Just shut up. It never mattered what I said. The two words I heard the most as a child were "shut up," so I did. Momma told me to shut up, Grandma, and Grandpa insisted I shut up, and later, the teachers, preachers, police officers, and foster parents all agreed that I should just shut up. Now I'm talking.

I'm Talking Now — Poem 1995

Born a storyteller.
Born as natural a storyteller as the rain is naturally wet.
Silenced early in her tumultuous childhood,
By secrets that weren't her own.
Secrets that begged she never tell.
Secrets that damned her soul to hell.
Secrets that lived behind their eyes.
Secrets they veiled with clever lies.
Secrets.
How they hold to one, they never should have owned.

How they cling to an innocent child, their tricks
unknown.
Secrets.
How very long they hid in me.
Now die old tales too long untold!
Damn yourselves and release your hold.
I'm talking now,
No more to be a closet closed so none will see.
A darkened hole, whose purpose wanes.
On now to life, and all good things.
I'm talking now.

Momma Ate Starch

When we lived with my grandparents, Momma tried desperately to have a moment of privacy, as we all did in a small house filled with sorrow. At night she'd go to bed early with me, but she would not go to sleep sometimes for hours. She'd smoke while reading murder magazines and she loved to elaborate on what she read. She gave me details about the victims, the bodies, the weapons, and the bad guys. Even more annoying than the running commentary would be her constant crunch, crunch, crunching. Momma ate Argo Starch. Yes, starch, the stuff you put in the wash to make your shirts crisp.

Ida Ruth, a woman my grandmother had come in and iron for her on and off for years, introduced Momma to Argo Starch. Ida

Ruth worked in exchange for food or hand-me-downs most of the time since money was scarce. I didn't feel invisible around Ida Ruth; she had the most reassuring open smile I ever saw. When Ida Ruth smiled, I could breathe easier, stand taller, and laugh deeper. Ida Ruth was truly remarkable. I hope someone told her that, at least once.

She had a daughter my age and I loved to play with her; I looked forward to her visits until grandma decided it didn't look right for me to be seen outside playing with a colored child. Ida Ruth brought her daughter a few more times and she'd sit and glare at me. I knew she hurt but I couldn't do anything about it, being just a six-year-old worthless white trash girl. The rules were made long before she or I ever drew our first breath. In those days, girls, especially poor black or white trash girls, sure seemed destined for damnation. Best you accept it, best you just swallow the soap, best you don't even let on that you question it at all. You ain't nothin' but cept a girl.

I have no idea why Ida Ruth ate starch. She said that lots of colored people did. Today we have starch in spray cans, but then it came in a little box in broken, odd-shaped pieces that looked like chalk. Ida Ruth would dissolve several pieces in water inside an empty RC Cola bottle. She'd shake the mixture vigorously and then insert a stopper, a cork with an aluminum sprinkler on the top, into the bottle. Then she'd stand in Grandma's kitchen at the ironing board hour after hour and sprinkle, iron, sweat, sprinkle, iron, sweat, and sing.

Grandma said Momma shouldn't eat Argo starch and forbid her to do so. She said Ida Ruth and her kind could because they weren't like us. So in order to keep it a secret from Grandma, Momma ate Argo starch in bed at night. The crunching drove me up the wall. I'd beg her to stop then she'd slap at me with her sticky, chalky fingers and tell me to shut up and go to sleep. That's what I wanted *her* to do.

Rage Comes Knocking

Momma and I lived next to Stink Creek for a while. The creek ran by the mill and through the village. An old and decrepit men's boarding house sat on the main highway, a stone's throw from our little house. Most of the boarding house residents were old drunkards, and it didn't take long for Momma to pick up one of the losers. He'd bring her booze and cigarettes and sometimes a piece of candy for me. Momma went to his place a few times, but, usually, he came to our house, where he'd sit on our old sagging couch, perched there like he actually belonged. The crusty old man smelled like a goat, a sickening combination of sweat, liquor, and cigars. He frightened me, and I stayed clear of him, as best I could.

One night, I had gone to bed and Momma sat playing solitaire at the kitchen table, which she often did for hours. She wasn't drinking, or I'd have stayed up, ever vigilant. I always had to

46

stay awake when Momma drank to make sure she didn't drop a lit cigarette when she nodded off; it was a survival thing. A child of an alcoholic has a full-time job just staying alive long enough to get a life. I had just begun to drift off to sleep, moments from sweet oblivion when the banging began.

Banging had never been good news. I scrambled out of bed like a boy soldier ready to do battle with whatever terror had broken the night. I ran into the kitchen just as Momma grabbed an iron skillet in one hand and yanked the cord attached to the ceiling light with the other, plunging us into darkness. Momma whispered to me: "Be real quiet and he'll go away." I didn't move a muscle; I listened to the swish, swish sound made by the ceiling light bulb as it swung back and forth over our heads.

From the kitchen doorway we watched the old man's hulking shadow through the glass on the front door. Momma was trembling and I was wheezing. My asthma always flared up at times like this. The drunken, angry man screamed, "Bitch! You dirty bitch, open this damned door! You can't use me like this, damn you. I ain't nobody's patsy, open this door or so help me, I'll kick it in."

He kicked and pounded. Each time his big fist hit home the glass windowpanes would rattle and threaten to shatter. Then a huge knife came through the glass, the biggest knife I had ever seen. I know now that it was a machete; then, I just saw a damned big knife. Realizing hiding and being quiet would not save us; Momma shoved me out the back door and screamed, "Run!"

She didn't have to tell me twice. I ran like a scalded cat. I crawled through bushes, slipping and sliding in mud, and scrambled up the front steps to a neighbor's house. Panting and wheezing I sat on a chair peering out into the dark night while our neighbor went up the street to the only house on the block that had a phone and called the police. Waiting to find out if Momma had survived was the worst of it. Unable to stop trembling, I felt like I might shake clean apart, and the lady of the house would just sweep the pieces up into a dustpan and toss them out into the yard.

Finally, a policeman came to the door and said they had arrested the man, and that Momma was home and just fine. He said I could stop crying and that I was safe, that all would be okay now. He had no idea how wrong he was; there might be safe moments, but there were few safe days.

I dried my tears and went home. After we swept up the glass and put a chest of drawers against the broken door, and after Momma promised me for the twelve- hundredth time in my short life that she'd never drink again, we went to bed. Sleep did not come a second time that night.

Frostbite

I had been playing the "finders keepers – losers weepers" game with Momma for some time. A dangerous game, but playing it made me feel like I had some power. I worked hard to be the finder, and, therefore, making Momma the weeper. Whenever I found

Momma's booze, I poured it out. I became as clever at finding her stash as she at hiding it.

On this particular day that dogs my memory, I found her hidden treasure and dumped it. As usual, she went into a rage when she realized what I had done. She slapped me around the kitchen and snatched me up by my hair. I shoved her as hard as I could, and while she recovered her balance by grabbing the edge of the kitchen counter, I locked myself in the bathroom. Momma banged on the door and cursed me for a minute or two and then got quiet, too quiet.

When my curiosity overcame my fear, I slowly ventured out of the bathroom. I found the back door wide open and Momma gone. It was freezing outside, and she had not taken her coat. Yet I did not feel terribly concerned, certain that the cold would drive her right back in as soon as her red-hot temper tantrum started to ice over.

When the better part of an hour had passed and she hadn't returned, I started to worry. I went to several neighbors' houses but she had not gone to any of them. Panicked, I ventured out under the heavy, dark gray skies. I crisscrossed the woods behind our house looking for her and calling her name. I found her passed out, leaning against a downed tree with an empty pint of vodka between her legs, several discarded cigarette butts and little white filters lay scattered all around her. Dressed in thin polyester slacks and a light sweater, her pants hiked up above her short socks, she had no protection from the day's cutting cold.

We sometimes picked rabbit tobacco in that area, an herb that grows wild in the South. Momma would dry and smoke the white tobacco when she ran out of packaged cigarettes or regular tobacco to roll. She had apparently outsmarted me this time and had stashed a back-up bottle in the woods. She probably used the downed tree as a landmark for her cache. Life would be easier if drunks were stupid. Unfortunately, most of the ones I have known are too clever for their own good.

Momma lay very still, like a toppled statue lying where it had fallen, and she was blue. I could not rouse her and I feared she might be dead. Her skin felt like an Eskimo Pie still in the slick cold wrapper. I ran crashing through the leafless winter brush to a neighbor's house. I knew the lady who lived there was a nurse. Everyone in the neighborhood was fed up with Momma and her little dramas, but when I told this lady I thought my momma might be dead, she agreed to come with me.

The two of us managed to half carry and half drag Momma back to our house. The neighbor stripped off Momma's damp clothes and bundled her in blankets. She alternately put warm wash cloths on Momma's hands and feet. After what seemed an eternity, Momma opened her eyes and started groping about, looking for her bottle. When we told her what had happened and that she had almost died, she said, "I wish I had."

Through The Ringer

The day Momma got her hand caught in the ringer of an old washing machine hangs in my memory like a heavy rain cloud about to drop it's load. The machine only agitated the clothes and rinsed them and then you had to feed each sopping wet piece by hand through two wooden rollers to ring out the water. The rollers ran continually when the washer was plugged in. The washer had not originally been designed to operate that way, but over the years it had been transformed into a Frankenstein machine, made from parts of several junked models, pieces no doubt found like treasures at the local dump.

The tub stood on tall skinny legs and looked like half of a fifty-five-gallon drum that had been painted white many years before when the original owner proudly brought it home from Sears and Roebuck. Most of the paint had peeled off when my stepfather and Momma rented the old house where the rusty thing sat on the back porch. Although the appliance was temperamental and unattractive, Momma felt glad to have it. Anything was better than washing clothes in the tub or sink by hand.

Momma would fill the large tub with water and soap, add the clothes, and plug her in. Oh the noise that old thing made, but it agitated the hell out of the clothes. Then she'd drain the dirty water and fill the tub again to rinse. Sometimes if the clothes were especially dirty, she might have to fill and empty the tub several times. The back yard would be a flooded muddy mess on laundry day since the water hose emptied directly into the yard below our porch.

Once the clothes were clean, Momma would pull out a piece and feed one corner of the cloth into the ringer. Then she'd reach to the other side and take hold of the cloth as it came through the ringer and guide it, sometimes assisting by pulling or wiggling.

On this particular morning, Momma, already three sheets to the wind, fed her hand through the ringer along with a wet blouse. Fortunately, my stepfather Du jour happened to be nearby and snatched the plug out of the wall. I always wondered if such an experience was where the expression "put through the ringer" came from?

Momma's hand didn't seem to hurt her much that day, however the next morning, after she'd sobered up, she howled in pain. I pretended to sleep through the screaming of obscenities as she stomped about the house on the old floor planks, cursing God and man. Things were always worse the morning after.

Chapter Six - Broken Boughs

Pepperell Lake

Alabama summers brought sun and more sun, accompanied by suffocating degrees of humidity. We lived in Pepperell Mill Village, and Pepperell Lake was about a mile up the road. That mile seemed like ten on an especially vicious summer day. You'd think those of us born and raised there would become accustomed to the heat. No one ever seemed to. When my grandparents, and later my momma, had to go into the cotton mill during those scorcher days it was not uncommon for people to faint away, right there on the work floor.

Sometimes on one of those hot, airless days, Momma would walk with my sister and me to the lake so we could take a swim. My sister and I would start the walk jabbering about this and that. The farther we walked with that endless sun beating on our heads, the quieter we became. The asphalt along the highway would be steaming, buckling under the relentless summer heat. We felt like we were wilting and in danger of melting into the shimmering asphalt, oozing liquid into the earth.

Once we turned off the highway onto the dirt road that led to the lake, each step created a red dust cloud, encouraging us to hurry along to the cool water. The lake provided a great escape from the heat, and we'd laugh and play with wild abandon, energized by the cool relief. Although we were free and raucous, we respected the lake and her rules. We never swam out past the rope.

Every child from the village and surrounding areas had been taught since his or her first dip in Pepperell Lake to stay on the beach side of the rope that divided the lake into two parts. One half of the lake, the swimming section, was divided into three smaller parts. The larger section of the three made up the main swimming area, with an easy sloping embankment and a dirt bottom. I loved the way the wet earth squished between my toes. The remainder of the swimming area held two square concrete pools. The larger for less experienced swimmers and a wading pool for the toddlers.

Momma never learned to swim. She'd sit on the edge of the wading pool with the other mothers, smoking cigarettes and drinking sweet tea while she dangled her slender legs in the water. The other half of the lake, the section beyond the rope and considered off limits, was left untended and was home to fish, birds, and snakes. The caretaker of the property frequently dragged the section used for swimming. He made sure no debris drifted into the recreational area where a snake might linger, camouflaged by a limb or log. Snakes are a part of life in the South. Near the water you are always on the lookout for water moccasins and rattlesnakes might show up pretty much anywhere.

One day while my sister and I were frolicking in the water, a horrible thing occurred. I will never forget that boy's screams. He played in the water with his friends, and they had been out precariously near the rope. Looking back, I wonder if they were out so far to escape the disapproving stares of the others at the lake that day.

The boy swam fast under the water, attempting to stay ahead of a friend who playfully gave chase, and when the child resurfaced, he did so directly under a moccasin. Water moccasins are not social critters. Their babies are born alive and immediately take off to fend for themselves. Moccasins are natural loners and will not go out of their way to attack. They will avoid humans whenever possible. But when that little boy accidentally crashed right into that moccasin, she did what came natural. She bit the intruder over and over again until he became quiet and still.

The real sadness that day, and the source of my sorrowful memory wasn't solely because a child had died. The real horror came from what I heard the grownups say only minutes after the dead boy's tiny, golden brown body, glistening with beads of water catching the day's sunlight, was removed from the lake. The grown-ups laughed, some genuine, some nervous and uncertain, but they laughed.

One man said, "No big loss; one less nigger to put up with."

In response a big, red-faced man laughed with a crude snort, and said, "Hell, I didn't even know snakes liked dark meat."

I learned that day that not all snakes are belly crawlers. The two-legged ones can sometimes be meaner than the ones who slither and hiss.

Belly Crawler

In our family, adults preferred that children were neither seen nor heard, especially girl children. When Momma moved us back in with Grandma and Grandpa in the mill village *again,* my grandparents were obviously not happy about it. I tried to be as invisible as possible without actually disappearing, as I often felt in danger of doing. I kept my mouth shut, hoping that in doing so I'd be safe, that I might escape the worst of things.

On one memorable day, just another scorcher in Alabama, too hot to do much of anything, I was thrilled when Grandma suggested that we go fishing at Pepperell Lake, the same watering hole where the boy had died less than a year before. We loaded up in Grandpa's old black and white Chevy with our cane poles sticking out the window.

Five minutes later we were unloading our poles and gear from the car. As usual, we spread out along the bank and chose our own sure-fire lucky spot. We didn't dare speak above a whisper, and then only when absolutely necessary, because Grandpa insisted the fish could hear you and would go to the other side of the lake. It was just fine with me that no one talked. If no one talked then no one fought.

I ambled off by myself to find the place to catch the big one. I found an ideal spot where there were several big boulders. The rocks were tiered, and I easily climbed down to a large rock shelf that jutted out over the water. Perfect! I sat down on the edge of the shelf, the rock hot on my butt and bare legs.

What a great place, I know I'll get lucky here, I thought.

I swung my legs over the edge, and my feet dangled about a foot above the lake. I unhooked the fishhook from where I had it secured to my cane pole and fished a big wiggly night crawler out of the sweet pea can I kept my bait in. I proceeded to bait my hook.

That's when I heard him. The sound low, so quiet at first that I wasn't certain I had heard anything at all, so I listened carefully to be sure.

The next time left no doubt. I heard a faint clear rattle. I forced myself to turn very slowly and look over my left shoulder in the direction of the rattle, louder now. There under the rock, just above where I sat, a big ole' rattler lay coiled and fretful. My heart pounded so loud I was sure the snake could hear it. I didn't move. I sat frozen, my pole in one hand and a wriggling worm in the other.

I smelled the water, the sun, and the earthy aroma of the worm in my hand. Barely breathing, I waited and waited. It seemed an hour passed though I'm sure it was only a handful of minutes. My body ached due to my twisted position and my skinny bottom felt numb, but I sat frozen, afraid to even blink.

The long, fat worm I held between my thumb and forefinger struggled and wiggled in an attempt to escape my grasp and the noonday suns hot rays, fighting to return to the safety of the cool, dark earth. I wanted to go with him. I feared his wiggling would be enough to make the snake strike.

That ole' rattler was looking right at me through the slits of his sleepy, lazy eyes. Occasionally he'd start to rattle again, low and slow, rising one octave at a time until I felt certain he'd strike out at me, only to relax once again, quiet himself, and continue to observe me and the restless worm with disdain.

Finally, convinced that I was no threat to him or merely unworthy of any more of his attention, he turned and disappeared into a crevice in the rock, and I got the heck out of there. Once on top of the boulders, I stopped and looked back at my perch above the lake. There sat my sweet pea can full of worms. I didn't consider going after it. Then I remembered the night crawler in my hand. He still wiggled, oblivious to our narrow escape. I knelt by a bush and released him to the earth.

Over forty years later, I now live twenty-seven hundred miles away. I occasionally go back to the area to see family. I no longer call it home. On a recent visit I took my life-partner, Walt, to meet my brother David and his family. David still lives in Opelika near Pepperell Lake.

My brother, his wife, my nieces, my nephew, and Walt and I set out to go see what time, man, and nature, have made of Pepperell

Lake. We found the dirt road fenced off, no longer open to the public. My brother, being the sort of man who usually finds a way, led us on despite all obstacles. We parked in the back parking lot of a Wal-Mart Super-Center and cut through a small field to where the road resumed behind the locked gate. We strolled up the familiar road, each of us quiet, almost reverent, lost in our memories. I whispered to Walt, describing to him how it had once been. It seemed right to be quiet, respectful as if the place had recently passed away.

The concrete areas that made up the smaller swimming pools were still there, decayed and green with years of algae and pond scum. We found parts of the bathroom structures collapsed on the ground and overgrown with kudzu. The lake looked considerably smaller, maybe because I had been so small when I last visited and maybe due to the lack of care. It was swallowed up by waste, choked on rotted wood and time. I couldn't find the boulder area, and we didn't see any snakes. But my mind recalled as my heart remembered, and my nose reminded me of all that once occurred when as a little girl, I listened to man's cruelty on the day some mother's baby died. That memory gave way to another, sitting on a warm rock on my numb behind, as I faced that ole' rattler. I shuddered as I realized how my childhood had been a series of near misses, then smiled warm in the knowledge that now I am truly safe. I turned my attention from what was to what is, took my lover's hand and walked away from yesterday.

Momma's Fear

The first hint of any storm, the slightest distant rumbling or sound of thunder, a flicker of a lightning bolt, was all it took to fill Momma's eyes with terror. Every fiber of her being would announce the coming of the howling fury, which might or might not come. At the first hint of ill weather coming our way, Momma would frantically gather blankets, candles, and flashlights, and disconnect every electrical appliance in the house. She'd shepherd us under the kitchen table where we'd cling to one another, hyper-vigilant in our expectation of certain doom.

We crouched huddled in fear, like boy soldiers in a foxhole on foreign soil. At each flash of lightning or boom of thunder, we'd jump in unison, holding tighter to one another. Inevitably the storm would pass, and once the day became quiet and still again, we'd crawl forth from our makeshift shelter. It seemed to me that we were always at least a little disappointed that we'd survived. So, after all, it was just another day. For a while the day had been charged up and dangerous with uncertainty and raw possibility. Now we were forced to face the never-ending, unyielding, moment-to-moment reality of our existence with nowhere to hide.

No port could shelter us from the ongoing storm raging within. Momma had so much fear. Surviving her fear was a constant struggle, not only for Momma but anyone near her.

Pin Curls and Blow-Up boobs

Early most mornings, Momma would sit at the kitchen table with her little two-sided mirror propped up in front of her, one side regular and the other magnified. Surrounded by her beauty products, she'd set forth to transform the image of the woman she critically studied in the mirror's reflection. Momma's hair would be fastened tight to her scalp in tiny pin curls with black bobby pins, which she had put in the night before. She put a hair net over the curls to keep them in place while she slept. I never knew how she could stand it; the handful of times I tried to sleep in pin curls, I pulled them all out in the middle of the night in the name of sleep.

Momma could roll her hair in dozens of curls in a matter of minutes. Using her mirror and a glass of water with a comb in it, she'd dip the comb in the water and use it to wet a piece of hair, then twirl and pin it into place. When sober, this was a nightly routine. Momma could never afford to go to a beauty parlor to get her hair cut, so when her hair got too long, she'd cut a half-inch or so from each section before she pinned it tightly to her scalp. Since she wore her hair in such tight curls, the cut always looked pretty good.

Momma's morning work area wasn't complete without a cup of black coffee, a pack of cigarettes, an ashtray, and a book of matches. Once she had everything arranged just so, she'd begin the process of becoming acceptable to the world that judged her so harshly, although never as harshly as she judged herself. First, she'd apply the face cover, using a big stick of cake makeup. She'd put a large smear on each cheek, forehead, chin, and a couple on her throat, then use both hands to rub the makeup evenly over her skin. She always bought a shade too dark for her pale complexion and used way too much of it. You could see a dark line on her throat and around her hairline. Her shirt collars were stained, and her makeup would rub off on my clothes and skin when she hugged me.

The next step, a liberal application of blush, came from a little plastic box. Then she applied her mascara and finished with a dark red lipstick. With her face done, she'd remove the bobby pins from her hair and brush out her tight curls. When satisfied with her hairdo, she'd spray it with a huge fog of cheap hairspray. Momma's hair did not move all day.

She had very small breasts and often wore falsies, or when she had none, stuffed her bra with toilet tissue or socks. When I was seven, momma mail-ordered a special bra from the back page ads of one of her murder mystery magazines. It had little balloons in the cups. She'd use a long straw to blow up the balloons to the desired size. Momma was delighted with her magic bra, she could be a size thirty-four on the street in the daytime, go into the bathroom, whip out her trusty straw, and become a thirty-eight in an instant for an evening in the neighborhood bar.

Unfortunately, the balloons had a slow leak. I frequently would have to tell Momma she only had one boob, where, to my dismay in public places she'd whip out her straw and re-inflate.

Genell Lois was a beautiful woman, but she never knew it. Five foot 6 inches tall and always slender, she cleaned up pretty and could sometimes be downright dazzling. Momma had an infectious laugh and twinkling, dancing hazel eyes. She never saw herself as more than okay. There were times though that I saw her as nothing short of beautiful.

No Options

Having more, becoming more, achieving more, these things weren't realistic options for a mill village girl. Some topics were never mentioned in our home. Topics that I would later understand were seriously discussed by most families. For example, attending college never came up in conversation. No one spoke about the possibility of even attempting to acquire a higher education. Grandma and Grandpa never attended school, and Momma only went through part of the fourth grade. The idea of actually graduating from high school was a lofty prospect and not really considered a realistic or even desirable notion. We only attended school because momma really didn't like truant officers.

As a child I never saw a bankbook. No one used a bank. We had no extra money to save, and everyone paid as they went, or did without. People often used the barter system instead of cash. They'd trade services or possessions. One would repair his neighbor's car in exchange for part of a fresh dressed pig. People with automobiles gave rides for garden produce or labor, and so on.

I remember being fascinated by the insurance policy my grandparents had for their burial plots. The payment sheet and legal papers were kept in a long, brown envelope that hung on a nail on the wall behind the front door. My grandparents would put the $1.50 cash money in it each month as soon as they had it and the insurance man would come by every month and collect it. He'd take the envelope down from its nail, remove the money, and log the transaction on the enclosed card. Then he'd write the information in his large black binder. All the while grandma and grandpa and the rest of us would be glued to his every action. Awed by the official capacity of this businessman's visit to our little home.

The process intrigued me. The official envelope, the cash inside it, and the man who conducted business right there in our living room. Once, when I was home alone I slid a straight chair over the linoleum and sat it under the envelope hanging on the wall. I climbed onto the chair and managed to reach the very bottom edge of the prize I sought and wriggled it free of the nail.

I sat down on the chair, feeling powerful and knowing that if I were caught the switching I'd receive would be harsh indeed. I upended the envelope and inspected the contents, mesmerized by the uniformity of the insurance man's monthly written entries on the card. I fondled the one-dollar bill, one quarter, two dimes and one nickel that my grandmother had put in the envelope for the next collection while my heart pounded like a cat burglar. Knowing that I'd be plenty sorry if I were caught getting into grownups business, I hung the envelope back on the nail and returned the chair to exactly the spot I had taken it from. I pocketed a dime.

Other than my observing that one business transaction, no one prepared me for the world to come. Things that others seemed to just know were a mystery to me. I never knew that a penis was a penis and a vagina was a vagina. I grew up with a *cooter-snapper* and boys had *clucca-bils*. Pregnancy and menstruation were dirty, taboo subjects, rarely mentioned and always hushed around the children. So when I started my period, I thought for sure that I must have been dying.

Nor did we discuss politics or ideas. Most people listened to their pastor and voted accordingly. They simply did not question the church, the government, the doctor, the teacher, the law or the boss. Follow blindly, don't ask questions, and accept suffering as the Lord's will. Your reward will be in Heaven.

Rather than go to a dentist for checkups, we let the tooth rot and then Grandpa would yank it out with pliers. I often used a rag to wash my teeth. Toothbrushes, especially a new one, were rare. Toothpaste was available about as often as a new toothbrush. We used baking soda or nothing at all. I didn't know I should brush the back of my teeth until I went to the dentist the first time in my early twenties.

No one replaced a bald tire. You replaced a tire when it blew. If you asked questions, you were a pest, a nuisance, and you might get hurt. Reading anything other than the Bible, the local paper, especially the comic strips, murder or gossip magazines, was considered a waste of time. Arguing was preferred over discussion. New ideas were stupid and threatening. If you pushed a new idea too hard, you'd be accused of being possessed by or doing the work of, Satan, or being a communist.

No one helped me with my homework or cared if I had F's on my report card. No objections were raised when I quit school in the second month of the ninth grade. Having failed fifth grade, I was fifteen. You only went to school because the law made you, but you could do whatever you wanted once you turned fifteen.

I always felt stupid. I think most of my dim wittedness stemmed from low self-esteem and poor nutrition. In class, I'd be lost in my own world, trying to breathe without making embarrassing noises due to my asthma, worrying about what might be going on at home with Momma, or trying to ignore the hungry rumbling sounds my stomach would be making. I'd become so accustomed to being wrong that I couldn't even imagine what it would feel like to be right.

There were times that I'd be questioned or tested on a subject that I knew the correct answers to. I'd become so stressed upon being asked that my mind would go blank. I still have that problem. I often use my brother, David's, saying when I cannot access the right information: "Well, I sure wrecked that train!" Then, when I stop trying so hard to wrestle the information from my mind, it'll pop forth, often proceeded by a little drum roll and concluded with "Snake-eyes."

Mrs. Green

There were adults in my childhood who appeared to go out of their way to validate my worthlessness. One of the most damaging ones, Mrs. Green, I only knew in passing. Her son went to the same elementary school I'd go to whenever we lived in the mill village, and they attended one of the churches Momma would sometimes drag us to.

It was on one of those dreadful Sundays. Momma was working the preacher for assistance so we attended the morning service at a Baptist church in the mill village. I remember the long, scary walk down the aisle. Church had not yet started and quite a few people were still milling about. I felt conspicuous as I skulked past the good church folk, my eyes downcast, wishing Momma hadn't sat all the way up in the front. Peeking up from under my shaggy bangs, I could see her perched on a pew throne in a silent petition for charity and mercy.

Mrs. Green glared at me from the gossip circle where she stood clustered with several overdressed, severe-faced women, exuding the heavy scent of cheap talcum powder and mothballs. Most were obscenely overweight, and their bright floral frocks seemed to blend together, creating a blinding hillside of oddly colored and shaped flowers. Independently, these women could be venomous. Gathered together, they were deadly. My head down, I tried to pass them quickly. I heard Mrs. Green say, "That poor child, she's mentally retarded, you know?"

I did not know what she meant, but one thing I immediately understood; what she had said about me was not a good thing. I continued on, sat down next to Momma, and asked her what 'mentally retarded' meant. She answered unaware the impact her words would have on my life.

"Mentally retarded means crazy. Retarded people ought-a not live around other people because they ain't right in the head. They do dangerous thangs."

Now I understood why I had always been so uncomfortable around everyone, I was crazy. I told Momma what Mrs. Green had said about me, which really proved to be a crazy thing to do because Momma went wild and took off after her. Momma caused quite a rile in the old church that day. She called Mrs. Green an old fat cow with an ugly mouth and said she and her sidekicks in gossip, and the whole damned church, could shove their mean words and their assistance up their holy-roller asses.

In the long run, this worked out well. The preacher and his daughter brought over a big box of food later that day along with two bags of hand-me-down clothes and paid our past due rent. Momma accepted their charity graciously. Regardless of her comment that they shove it, she never looked a gift horse in the mouth.

I never once considered that Momma might have been defending me when she went crazy all over Mrs. Green in the Baptist church that day. It didn't occur to me for a moment that I might not be mentally retarded. Rather, I thought she became upset because the lady had told me the truth.

Throughout the years I'd often hear momma's words from the pew that day, "Mentally retarded means crazy. Retarded people ought-a not live around other people because they ain't right in the head. They do dangerous thangs." Whereupon I'd remind myself to be scarce, indirect, invisible, so people wouldn't realize what I was, and run me off.

Hubby Number Five

In 1964 Momma married her fifth husband, James Kelley. She got pregnant right away and soon after, James, who worked as a butcher at A & P Supermarket, was transferred to Tyler, Texas. We packed James' rusted out multicolored station wagon to the gills.

James tied the hood down with a wire clothes hanger and a matching hanger stuck out of the hole where an antenna had once resided, and off we went to the Promised Land.

Although ten years old, I only remember snippets of Tyler. Life with Momma was a chaotic roller coaster ride during the best days. The past year had been an especially impossible one for me. I'd been sick and in bed for months and had rarely attended school the whole year. In addition, Momma had moved us several times in the previous twelve months. As a result of the moves, Momma's nuptials, and my asthma, I flunked the fifth grade.

The year before Momma married James, she had some old doctor that she drug in from somewhere that would come to our house to give me a shot when my asthma would not relent. She rarely had any money to pay the man, yet he kept coming over, and he had me taking a daily medication called Tedral. An old man and very gray, the doctor's cold eyes peered out from beneath bushy eyebrows that dominated his slack and ashen face. He frightened me but I was so sick that any attention, any offer to help with the struggle for my next breath, was welcomed even if I dreaded his presence.

The scary old doctor overdosed me more than once, although it was only in hindsight that we realized that had happened. After he gave me a shot and determined that I might be in trouble, he'd have Momma hold me down while he drew blood from my groin, supposedly to check the blood gas levels. The unbearable pain would later prove to be unforgettable. After we settled into our new house in Tyler, Momma took me to a doctor there. He immediately took me off Tedral, which was illegal in Texas because it could be very addictive. The new doctor weaned me off the drug and I slowly got better.

In time, Momma had to accept the obvious. She had looked the other way because she could not pay the doctor and she always treated doctors like they were Gods. In her heart she had known that it wasn't right that she allowed that old man to be alone in a room with me. She should have said or done something. She never did. Often, after the old doctor would give me a shot, I'd drift off to sweet oblivion. That's all I know for sure. That's all I want to know.

James Kelley, was also asthmatic and a really weak spineless man. He made a huge mistake marrying my Momma because she abused him mercilessly. Don't get me wrong; James could be an asshole and Momma handled him like a pimp handles a whore. When drunk, even while pregnant, momma would physically attack James. She took a lot of the anger she had for other men out on him because he'd take it. They fought constantly. Sometimes it seemed Momma couldn't stand the sight of him. She'd walk by him while he sat quietly in a chair and say, "You useless bastard."

He'd counter with something equally charming like, "At least I'm not a drunk, pregnant whore," and it'd be on.

Sometimes James would leave for a few hours or even several days, but he always returned. On one occasion Momma would welcome him back with open arms and sweet words, and the next time she'd fly at him as soon as he walked through the front door, screaming, "You useless asshole! Where the hell have you been? What makes you think you can just walk back in here big as life?"

Life in Tyler, Texas, turned out to be only different from Alabama geographically. The next thing I knew, Momma and James were packing the station wagon in the middle of the night and ducking out on the landlord and bill collectors, again. At least that time we weren't handed a one-way ticket on public transit like when husbands numbers three and four sent us packing. No train, no bus, just Momma and James fighting all the way out of Texas and across Louisiana and Mississippi, and they were still arguing when we crossed back into Alabama, just another day. Leaving always seemed more natural for us than staying. Momma used to proudly proclaim that she must be part gypsy or nomad because she could always be out the door at a drop of the hat.

James did try to leave Momma a couple of times. Maybe I shouldn't say James left so much as Momma ran him off. Once, when we lived in the house with the old spindly-legged washing machine in Georgia, he left for eight days. We had no food and no money to buy any. Momma made crumbly biscuits and cornbread with mostly water, and we picked wild onions, which were good. One day we had tomato soup made with ketchup. When you're hungry, anything more substantial than air is good.

A couple of months later, James took us to an old cabin that one of his work buddies owned on a deserted lake. We went up for the weekend to fish. Momma managed to bring a bottle or two along without James knowing about it. We had just arrived at the cabin and were unpacking the station wagon, getting our poles strung up and the bait ready to go down to the lake when the next thing we knew, Momma was drunk as a skunk.

Momma didn't get drunk slowly. She'd be as sober as a judge one-minute, and swaying in the breeze the next. When James realized what she'd done, the arguing started full-bore, till momma hit him hard upside his head and he stumbled back over the open tailgate of the station wagon. James got up, slammed the tailgate, got into his car, and drove away.

He did not come back for three days. I thought we'd die in that cabin. Momma didn't worry that we had little food, no electricity, and an abundance of bugs and snakes to contend with, or that we were stranded in the middle of nowhere. She only concerned herself with the fact that her extra cigarettes were in James' car. She found some old cigar butts in the cabin, which she smoked and choked on. Momma was not in a pleasant mood.

I don't know why James came back. Maybe he feared that we'd die and he'd be held responsible for our deaths, or maybe he actually loved Momma. Whatever his reasons, I was glad to see him drive up that rutted dirt road with the red dust bellowing behind him.

The Revenuers

Occasionally James would take us to the woods to gather worms for fish bait. A magical process for a child. James would choose a small tree, five to six inches wide, and cut it off two to three foot above the ground. Then he'd find a rock that fit just right in the palm of his hand. Once pleased with the rock of his choosing, James would rake it back and forth across the top of the tree stump, creating a vibration that traveled down the trunk into the roots and on into the earth. This vibration would drive the night crawlers, which are some big-o-worms, out of the dirt. The next thing you know, worms are all around you, slithering to-and-fro.

My sister Deborah, Momma, and I would be giggling and gathering worms as fast as we could. We each had an empty tin can we'd fill in no time. Then we'd take the wriggling night crawlers home and kept them in a wooden framed box James had built and filled with dirt, so we'd have bait available whenever we wanted to go fishing. On this worm hunt though James' vibrations drew the attention of more than the night crawlers.

There we were filling our cans, James raking the rock back and forth on the stump when we heard the thunderous sound of booted feet crashing through the woods, heading toward us at breakneck speed. Before we had a chance to spit, we found ourselves surrounded by five men, their rifles leveled on us. We were all terrified, and even Momma was speechless for once. One of the men, the one in front and clearly the boss, said they were Revenuers, government agents out to bust bootleggers.

After a lot of hollering, they finally lowered their weapons. Apparently the bootleggers in the area used the vibration technique to warn one another when the Revenuers were in the woods, giving their buddies an opportunity to hide their moonshine and get away. Yep, life with hubby number five was a real hoot.

Chapter Seven - Twigs

Steps — Halves —Wholes and Temporaries

I find the question, "Do you have siblings?" hard to answer. My sister Deborah, who is eighteen months older than I, was the only sibling I really lived with for any real amount of time. Next came my sister Doreen, who was created in my daddy's second marriage, born when I was eight years old. I did not have an opportunity to meet her until I was fourteen, I do not really remember being aware that she even existed.

My brother, David Mark, joined the family just after I turned eleven. By that time I rarely lived with momma. I went in and out of foster homes for a year when twelve, and spent six months at my daddy's in California at fourteen. I married the first time at fifteen. So I was not raised with my brother David.

When I went to California in 1969, I met my stepbrother and sister, John and Anne, the children of my stepmother Lynda, my daddy's third wife. There also were the temporaries, like the four kids in Detroit when Momma married husband number four, and Momma's fifth husband's two sons from a previous marriage that stayed with us a few times.

We are not the typical family. Yet, this sort of family is more common than most people care to admit. We are steps and halves and wholes and occasionally temporaries, like one another or not, interact or ignore, cherish or despise, we are family.

Deborah Bathsheba - February 21, 1952

The only one of my five siblings that I grew up with, well at least partially, would be my sister Deborah. Momma moved us constantly, and sometimes when she moved out of our grandparent's house Deborah would stay with our grandparents and I'd go with Momma, being the youngest. There were times that I wouldn't see Deborah for weeks or months, and later on it stretched into years.

Of all my siblings Deborah and I should be the closest. We shared the same foxhole so to speak, yet we have never been close. Deborah bullied me. Sometimes I thought she hated me and I know she resented me. As a child I did not understand, but now I know that I was the only person Deborah felt she had power over. The only one weaker, younger, and more frightened than her. My terror made her feel brave. My weakness made her feel strong.

Deborah suffers from manic depression, which was very apparent even in her childhood years if anyone had actually been paying attention. In 1990 a therapist diagnosed her with a multiple personality disorder. I had no trouble believing this. Deborah talked non-stop and lied even when the truth would do just as well. If you dared to confront her, she'd argue with you and insist she was right, even in the face of undeniable evidence to the contrary.

She'd argue until you tired and gave in, or she'd storm away, cursing you, and never, and I mean *never*, admit she even might be slightly wrong. As a young girl and teenager, she'd simply go to sleep when she didn't get her way or to avoid the truth. She could escape into sleep and would not wake up even if you shook her and yelled, she appeared to have literally left her body.

Throughout the years, on the rare occasion that Deborah and I would discuss the past, I'd bring up some of these occurrences. She always denied any of it ever happened. After her MPD diagnoses, I wondered if she really didn't know? There were definitely several personalities involved.

I thought she just rewrote things to make them more acceptable to her. We deal with our pain in our own ways. Now I wonder if the person I saw *doing* the action or heard *saying* the words was the same one I confronted regarding it? If not, how cruel I must have seemed to her? I think from the day of her birth, my sister simply tried desperately to be seen and heard, but Daddy was avoiding home and a drunken wife by the time Deborah was born, and Momma was nursing a vodka bottle and had no time to nurse a baby. So Deborah cried; she's crying still.

David Mark- January 16, 1965

Against all odds and Momma's desperate prayers to God, my little brother David was born on January 16, 1965. Momma stayed drunk during most of her pregnancy and smoked one Old Gold cigarette after another. In addition, we had moved to Texas and then back to Alabama during the third through the seventh months of her pregnancy, an extremely hard journey.

She took several doses a day of B.C. or Goody Powders for her constant headaches. B.C. and Goody powders are aspirin in powder form that come folded in paper bindles. Momma would pour the powder from the bindle directly into her mouth. I tried it once, and found it awful; I don't think she had taste buds or a gag reflex anymore.

Momma didn't want another baby. She didn't want the two she already had. Like she had done to me ten years prior, when drunk Momma would beat her stomach with her fists, trying desperately to kill David. Her outrageous, abusive behavior was not as shocking to me as you might think it should have been, as my image of children and birth were skewed by her statements often expressed to me for as long I can remember.

When drunk, Momma would tell me how she had tried time and time again to kill me in her womb. She blamed me that she drank, that my daddy left us, that we were dirt poor, and that she was sad. Therefore, of course, it was my fault that she hit me. If only I had died, her life would have been great. It was my fault, all of it. I felt guilty and responsible for so much pain, and this added greatly to my desire to be invisible.

I didn't die though, nor did my beautiful baby brother. For a long time I wondered whether this was a good thing. Today when I look at my nieces and my nephew, I'm grateful David survived to create such fantastic children. I'm grateful David survived so I can love him and his wife of twenty plus years; I'm grateful he survived to love me. Unfortunately, David did not completely avoid damage; none of us did. You don't show up whole when you enter through a toxic womb.

My baby brother emerged from our momma's womb with a huge red mole in the center of his forehead. It looked like a blood clot. The doctors removed it shortly after his birth. I don't know what caused it, but whenever I saw the scar left from its removal or thought of it, and when I think of it now, I see Momma beating her stomach, and my heart cries for the baby I couldn't protect. As an adult, David has had serious neurological problems and three minor to moderate strokes, all before his thirty-fifth birthday.

Momma left James, David's father, soon after she gave birth to David, and moved us into another choice apartment in Opelika. I was twelve years old. She managed to stay drunk throughout most of David's infancy. David would be hungry and wet, and Momma would be passed out and wet. For a while I stole milk off the neighbor's porch in the early morning hours. I never heated it or sterilized the bottles. I did not know what to do. Once, when David may have been eight months old, Momma woke up, came to, and found him gnawing on a chicken leg I had given him. She went nuts and said I was trying to kill him. I had no idea how to care for a baby, or myself, for that matter. I just had to do something.

Doreen - March 3, 1963

After Daddy divorced Momma he remarried. This time he did his wife shopping a little closer to home and chose a local girl from Half Moon Bay, California. On March 3, 1963, they had a little girl. Doreen was an amazing little beauty with golden hair and big green eyes. Born with a developmental disorder, Doreen had to wear a brace apparatus on her legs every night when she was put to bed. The brace was terribly painful and Doreen hated having to wear it but had to if she were to ever walk properly. Regardless of life's efforts to hobble her right from the gate, Doreen grew up tough, smart, beautiful, and unpredictable.

At eleven years old, you'd find her ripping along on a dirt bike, or driving her stepfather's motorboat on the lake. In her teens she was no stranger to the drugs, gangs, and party life of San Jose, California, where she was raised as an only child after our daddy and her mother were divorced in January 1964 when Doreen was ten months old.

The following year Daddy married his third and final wife, Lynda, on April 29, 1965. That would make a total of three marriages for my daddy, and my mother managed to tie and untie the knot seven times. That's a perfect ten between the two of them.

Chapter Eight - Kindling for the Fire

The Bootlegger - 1967

Twelve, almost thirteen, and in my mind I was all grown up. A natural loner, I was pleasantly surprised when I actually hit it off with Lori-Lyn, a girl I met at another *new* school I attended for a few weeks. Since I never had friends, my relationship with Lori-Lyn was a new and exciting experience for me. We had one very important thing in common which made us fast allies. She and I had the same secrets behind our front doors. Doors changed frequently but the secrets behind them stayed the same. In both of our homes everyone stayed drunk most of the time. I could never have a friend, even if I lucked out and made one because I had too many secrets. The biggest one waited behind the front door of whatever home we lived at the moment.

I worried constantly when at school or anywhere except home. I feared what might be going on. I'd rush home and then freeze before I crossed the threshold, needing to know, dreading what I might find. I didn't dare take anyone home, ever. Lori-Lyn and I could be friends though because her parents were drunks too.

On a sunny Saturday I visited Lori-Lyn's home for the first time. Her house was a typical Southern poor man-style. Small with a big porch and no railings, the paint was peeling off in long strips.

Old rusty cars and appliances ornamented the yard; a lot like the places Momma usually rented, just the basics because everything is always temporary. I felt right at home.

Lori-Lyn and I sat side by side on the weathered porch planks with our feet hanging over the edge, swinging our legs to-and-fro, and chattering, as teenage girls will do. There were four boys in Lori-Lyn's front yard, shifting from foot to foot, awkwardly attempting to talk to us.

Oh what fun. Now I had a friend, we were talking to boys, and my Momma wasn't there. I thought, *what a wonderful day!* If I'd had any idea how that day would turn out, I'd gladly have run back to Momma and a hungry baby just as fast as my spindly legs would carry me. I didn't know; you never do see monsters coming.

So I stayed and giggled, wiggled and played. Late that afternoon, an older man drove up in a big white-paneled truck. All the adults became very animated. It was obvious that this man was important. The new man and Lori-Lyn's father unloaded several heavy wood crates from the truck, and then they went inside and started seriously partying. The music and whooping and hollering mingled with drunken slurs, and the usual arguments, poured at varying volumes out the open windows and doors. It felt normal to me, just like home.

Later, as the lightnin' bugs and mosquitoes gathered, the man from the truck that I'd later refer to as the Bootlegger, stumbled out onto the porch and sat down with Lori-Lyn and me. There were still a couple of boys hanging around, and this older man made us kids feel important. Adults didn't waste any time with children in my world, so his attention really made me feel grown up.

The stranger had a quart jar of moonshine and offered it to us. I had taken a swig from Momma's bottle many times. Sometimes I did it to piss her off or to try and make it less for her to get drunk on. I had even started experimenting with it to escape the pain and fear I felt, but I never had enough booze to get really hammered.

When the stranger passed the jar of moonshine around, we all tried a sip, because that was all you could take. Home brewed country moonshine, and well over one hundred-proof; it could take the tar off the roof. We cringed and gagged, but kept our composure as well as kids can because we didn't want to blow this great opportunity to party with the big boys.

Slowly regaining consciousness several hours later, I stumbled out of a dense fog that I had never experienced before. When I managed to surface, I found myself in the cab of the Bootlegger's truck. I opened my eyes just a smidgen, cautiously reentering consciousness. Barely dawn, the sky slightly pink as the sun slipped into place to start a new day. I felt bruised, sore, and sick. I took a deep breath to steady my now pounding heart and fully opened my eyes and pulled them from the sky I saw through the nasty windshield, down past the steering wheel, where I found myself face to face with a monster. I screamed until the monster's huge hand clamped roughly over my mouth.

The Bootlegger made it clear that I could have it one of two ways, with or without his beating me within an inch of my life. These had been my only options. I thought he'd finish with his brutality, and abandon me where we were, or maybe have a bit of conscience, and drive me back to my neighborhood. Tragically however, that was only the beginning of the nightmare.

He took me with him to his place in Tennessee. We stayed in what now reminds me of a housing project, in a tiny two-story apartment. The kitchen and living room were downstairs and the only bedroom and bath were upstairs. Twenty-four-seven the drunks would come and go, buying moonshine, drinking, talking, laughing, gambling and fighting.

The Bootlegger had a filthy recliner that he lounged in like a king. He always had a bottle of shine or a beer between his legs and a cigarette in his hand, and a large handgun never left his side. His nails were filthy, and the fingers of his right hand, where he held his cigarette, were permanently stained yellow from nicotine.

I tried to stay out of sight as much as possible. While the adults partied downstairs, I sat in the dark stairwell, unseen, listening, trying to hear what was going on and to decide what I should do, what I could do. Twice I attempted to escape when the adults were passed out and things quieted down, and both times I got caught. The front door had two deadbolts and a chain because bootleggers require security to avoid being robbed or busted. Trapped, I waited, listened, cried.

Being held in this filthy shit hole for at least ten to twelve days, I lost track of time. All I knew for sure was that I was scared, hurt, hungry, and filthy. I spent a lot of time sitting in a corner of the bedroom, or behind the bedroom door, with my legs pulled up to my chest and my arms wrapped tightly around them. I'd rock and cry very quietly so I didn't attract anyone's attention. I had watched men do this sort of thing to Momma, but until now I had managed to avoid the worst of it. I discovered quickly that I would be punished and even more abused if I drew attention to myself. The Bootlegger would get especially angry if I cried or begged.

So when anyone was watching I made myself sit still and quiet – but when alone – I let the tears roll and rocked and held myself in a childish attempt at self-comfort. There was no comfort to be had, no God, no knight in shining armor, and no mercy. I crouched in dark corners listening, listening so hard my ears hurt, hearing every breath they took, every move they made, the swearing, fighting, the disgusting jokes, and the awful laughter. Laughter is not always a good thing. Sometimes it's just not funny.

I didn't dare shower because that would definitely draw attention. The bathroom was so dirty that I'm not sure I would have stepped into the shower even if it had been safe, and there was no way that I would ever have sat in the tub. No toilet paper or linens were to be found, so I washed a dirty washcloth several times with soap and hot water. I'd use it, wash it, and reuse it, over and over again. I hid it under the sink so no one else would take it. It's strange how important that ratty old washcloth became to me.

Homecoming

One night, late, the Bootlegger told me, "Git yore crap girl and come on."

I could only hope that he was taking me home. In his many drunken rants, I had overheard him say that he had to make another delivery to Opelika soon, so as I climbed into his truck I thought to myself, *please make today the day*. We drove all night. I stayed against the door and as quiet as a secret thought. I didn't dare ask him where we were going.

Just before sunrise he pulled off onto an old logging road and raped me again, and yes, it is rape even if you don't fight. I don't know why, but I wanted to live, and I didn't want to be beaten and battered on top of everything else. I discovered early on that the more I struggled or said, the meaner he'd get. So I lay limp, lifeless, my face turned as far away from him as possible, so I would not see him or smell his awful breath.

When finished with me, the Bootlegger drove another hour or two, talking non-stop about what would happen to me if I ever told anyone anything. "Besides, he said, "No one will believe a little tramp like you; you ain't nothin' but white trash."

He dropped me off on the highway two blocks from my grandparents' house in the village; I didn't want to go to Momma's place; I figured she'd be drunk and passed out anyway, and I needed help. I had no idea what I'd say to my grandparents, I just felt so grateful to be home and alive, and I felt certain that they must have been worried sick about me.

I rushed up the front steps and onto the porch, but just before I reached the front door, Grandma snatched it open and came at me in a rage, her face twisted into a vicious snarl as she screamed, "You're just like your momma, a no-good drunk whore, and I ain't putting up with it no more."

She said Momma was in Lee County Hospital and added through bared teeth spitting venom, "You go on up there and stay with your sorry ass momma. Y'all are two peas in a pod, and I don't want nothin' to do with yall's craziness no more."

Having had her say, my grandmother slammed the door in my face. For several minutes I stood frozen on the porch, stunned. I struggled to understand. I couldn't believe that after trying so desperately to get home, after attempting to escape, to survive, after the joy of seeing my grandparents' house again and visualizing that safety and sanity might exist in the world, that I was brutally attacked again, this time with words. I just stood there.

Still I can see myself, then, in that place. It all looks like a scene from a movie, all slow motion and black and white. I stood frozen, unable to understand what had just happened. Not all rapes occur between the legs; some happen between the ears, and are painful, undeserved penetrations of the heart. Slowly, I accepted my

complete aloneness and set out down the highway. I had to get to
Lee County Hospital. Maybe just this once, Momma would be there
for me.

Lee County Hospital

The walk from my grandparents' house to the hospital
seemed to take hours although it was only one mile. Tired and
hungry, sore, confused, and heart-broken, each step felt like a
monumental effort. It turned out that Momma had been checked into
the hospital because of pleurisy and alcohol-induced delirium
tremens, better known as DT's. When I showed up, she let on very
little that she was aware that I'd been gone at all. I just hung out in
her room. I didn't tell her much, and she didn't ask.

I'd been there, sitting rigidly in a straight chair by her bed for
several hours when she finally asked why I was staying so long. I
told her that Grandma had kicked me out. I almost fell out of my
chair when Momma said, "It's your own damn fault. You ought-a-
not-a run off like you did; you had everyone worried sick. Now
you've gone and got yourself kicked out on the streets."

I said; "I'm sorry Momma, but what am I gonna do, I don't
got nowhere to go."

Momma shook her head wearily, seemed to resign herself to
the obvious and replied, "Well, I can't help you, I'm sick. I guess
that as long as the nurses don't put up no fuss, you can just stay
here."

I said: "Okay, Momma." It wouldn't have done any good to say more.

Momma shared a room with a woman who worked as a maid for an upper class lady named Stella, from Auburn. Auburn is right next to Opelika, just a couple of miles from the mill village. The two towns are called the twin cities and that's where the common ground ends. The two cities couldn't be more opposite. Auburn's a college town and had always been off limits for a mill village girl, and the college crowd wanted nothing to do with Opelika and the cotton mill people.

This up-town lady, Stella, came up to see her maid twice a day. I met her the first day, and when she came the next morning she saw me sleeping in the lobby. She returned after dinner and became suspicious when she saw me sharing my Momma's meal tray. Stella asked if I was okay and Momma told her my grandma had kicked me out and I had nowhere to go. The next morning, Stella brought buttermilk biscuits with bacon in them. She returned midday with fried chicken and more biscuits.

She tried to talk to me, but I felt incapable of communication. My mind kept playing reruns of the past two weeks in graphic detail. When I'd finally fall into a fitful sleep in the chair or in the lobby, I'd awake in terror, back in his truck, smelling his stench as he plunged into me like I had no worth other than his twisted pleasure. In shock, ashamed, and fully aware that I could never tell anyone what happened to me, never. He was right, no one would ever believe white trash like me.

I desperately wanted a bath and a bed, I felt like garbage, refuse. I still had his disgusting filth all over me, inside me; I wore him. I knew I'd never be clean again, even if you turned me inside out and scrubbed me raw with turpentine. I had no trust left and feared that if Stella butted in, she'd get me kicked out of the hospital, and then I'd really be alone.

In less than two weeks I'd been kidnapped, repeatedly raped, beaten and starved, kicked out of my grandparents' house, and had found my Momma in the hospital. I don't know if I could have told Grandma the truth, even if she had given me the opportunity, but I had thought she'd need to know what had happened to me, where had I been, why I'd left, why I didn't call? I even thought my grandparents might have informed the police that I was missing. I later learned that Momma's neighbors had told my grandparents that I'd been over at Lori-Lyn's house partying with boys, and I had voluntarily run off with a man in a truck.

I wonder if I had never returned, would they have ever called the police or considered that just maybe I'd been taken against my will, or would they have just been glad to have one less person to rescue and one less mouth to feed?

It took a few days, but Stella finally convinced me to go home with her. I will never forget the first night at her house; I took three baths and several showers. I felt much better but still dirty. Some stains soap cannot wash away.

Demons and Exorcisms

Stella had two young sons and a beautiful home in downtown Auburn, near the university where her husband worked. The boys were nice enough to me but distant. Stella was a devout Christian, and for a while I found comfort in her faith, comfort that quickly faded. I had been a guest in their home for two weeks when her husband accused me of being possessed by demons because I didn't wear a bra. He said it was my fault that he felt lust for me. Stella defended me, but I saw their religion in a different light after that.

Raised knowing a cruel, punishing, vengeful God, one who created beings that he was supposed to love, and then he'd send them to burn in hell for eternity. In my family, community, and a multitude of different churches and foster homes, I had seen, time and time again, people say one thing and do another, and mankind rationalize almost any awful thing in the name of God. Even the bootlegger had gone on and on about how much he loved Jesus. At thirteen years old, I had seen enough to doubt the existence of such an indifferent master. If God did exist, I could not understand why he'd allow such terror to be inflicted on a child?

I had witnessed one exorcism when a Pentecostal preacher insisted that he could cure Momma's alcoholism. I had also been present when people were speaking in tongues on two occasions when I visited a neighbor kid's church years before. I suppose I'd been hopeful that a well-to-do lady's God would be different, kinder, actually forgiving and loving, as I had so often been told he was, yet had never witnessed. I quickly lost interest in Stella's religion though; I came to see her faith as just another all too familiar case of obsessive fanaticism.

Her husband drank a lot, and Stella avoided dealing with him and anything else unpleasant by hiding behind a plastic smile and Jesus. Like a wind-up toy, no matter what happened, she just smiled that strange smile and quoted Scripture. Several years later, her husband killed himself.

I stayed with Stella and her perfect rich, white, Christian family for a month, and then I was passed on, like the latest ice cream flavor. Stella sent me to live with her friend from church, Sarah. Sarah was a good woman but deeply scarred. After a brief stay first at Sarah's, I went on a little tour of the local foster system. I lived in each household for four to eight weeks on average, a total of eight foster homes in all. All were religious extremists, and two had been pastors and their families.

In each home they'd welcome me with that plastic smile and tell me how the Lord had led them to come into my life and rescue me. The first opportunity, usually a Sunday, they'd parade me around their church, making sure everyone knew what great Christians they were for taking me in and saving me from the hands of Satan. Inevitably they'd insist that I be baptized in their church so the Lord would wash away my sins, which they were quick to list, and to ensure that my wretched soul would be saved and therefore spared eternal damnation.

I appreciated their concern over the condition of my soul, but I'd argue that I had already been baptized several times in thirteen years. Each time Momma would drag us to church for *charity,* the church would dunk me. But the next church always denounced my previous baptisms and insisted that *their* ceremony in *their* church was the only sure thing. In foster homes the baptisms continued. I would be baptized in one home, and a few weeks later I'd be moved to a different home, usually within a few miles of the previous one. Frequently the families that the county placed me with were of the same faith, most often Baptist, if not Baptist then Methodist, which made it even more confusing, when I would inevitably receive the same speech.

They insisted that I must be baptized in their church; the ones before did not count. I think I was just entertainment for these poor, often illiterate, boring little communities. They liked the show, and the preacher enjoyed the opportunity to tell my story, my sad little secrets, in front of the congregation. It seemed to give everyone a real kick in the shorts. Good stuff, big sinner in a small town church. As a kid I didn't know if they were trying to save me or drown me, but I was squeaky clean and had a stack of little Bibles with my name written in them. They weren't important to me. Books can't hug you, and you can't eat them.

Daily home life with these people was always the same. They got the county checks, and I stayed out of the way. Fortunately, I had a lot of experience in being invisible. I found it best to only show up at chore time, mealtime, and the dog and pony show called Baptism. A few of the homes would have four or five foster kids and two or three of their own children, who were referred to as the real kids. All of us fosters would be piled on top of each other in one room and fed at a separate table. The real kids had better clothes, nicer rooms, and definitely bigger plates of food.

Anyone who caused trouble or questioned the pecking order was usually gone in a day or two. More than once I had to quickly pack my brown paper bag so they could drive me to the next temporary home. There were plenty of needy kids to replace you and therefore, the county-check. A new kid brought excitement and praise for the foster parents from their peers, we were small town entertainment. Then if you didn't work out, your foster parents could always blame your dismissal on Satan. Lord knows you can't save "em" all.

I eventually accepted that no place was better or worse than any other place, so I went back to live with Momma. At the time, she attended a day rehabilitation program for mentally and emotionally handicapped adults near the old viaduct in Opelika and lived in a tiny little trailer in a run down trailer park. She sat at a table all day in a barn-like building with many people who, for the most part, weren't able to speak or communicate. A few were actually strapped into their chairs and just parked for the day, simply housed until the bus came to take them home.

Momma did art projects and ceramics. One day she brought home three little ceramic ball and glove pieces she had made. The balls were separate from the gloves, and each ball had one of our names written on it. "Tony" was written on mine, "Tony," not "Toni," which is my name.

Momma insisted she had made it, but I knew she'd had someone else do it. Even the world's worst mom couldn't misspell their own child's name and then not even notice the mistake before she gave it as a gift, could she? I'd think, 'Hey can you see me?' Maybe I really am invisible.

Carhop

I'd been home with Momma for less than a month when due to her failure to pay the rent, we were asked to vacate our residence. The trailer in Opelika had been unbearably small but the next one was even worse, a one-room trailer with an obscenely small bathroom. An ancient silver round-bubble that you pulled behind a car. It was meant for camping, not living. Momma said, "Hush up, it's only temporary." Everything was always temporary.

Some charity had given us a box of hand-me-down clothes and I found a beautiful Cinderella dress, my size, in the box. I never seemed to find anything that would fit my bony featureless body and I never wore a dress, but even a bony tomboy at some point wants to, needs to, look pretty. After all I was a teenager and my hormones were raging.

The beautiful black dress fell just above my knees. Made of a clingy chiffon material, it hugged my hips and breasts in a flattering way and had see-through full-length sleeves that buttoned with tiny delicate buttons at the wrist. The pretty dress made me feel visible.

I would have looked foolish and out of place in that dress even if I'd been dining at a high end restaurant with fancy folk having a gourmet candlelit dinner, complete with expensive champagne in crystal stemware because I was too young for it. But I must have really been a sight walking down the highway in my Cinderella dress, old tennis shoes, straight stringy hair, and my bangs hanging limp in my eyes.

It's beyond me where I ever got the idea to ask for a job at the drive-through burger restaurant on Pepperell Parkway, on the border of Opelika and Auburn, since it served as a hangout for university kids. Definitely not my scene, if I had had one, a universe I had never been part of. Emboldened by my pretty dress, I walked in and asked for a job. I had no work history, no social skills; no clothes appropriate to wear, and very poor hygiene. Most importantly, I was not of legal age to employ. In addition to my more obvious shortcomings, I couldn't look anyone in the eye, and I shuffled nervously when I spoke.

So you could have knocked me over with a thimble when the manager actually hired me. At the time I felt sure that he believed I was fifteen because I looked so mature and beautiful in my Cinderella dress. But more likely he was hoping to take advantage of me, as he attempted to do just that on more than one occasion. I didn't care why he hired me really; I had a job!

I'd make tons of money, especially in tips, so I thought. I was sorely mistaken. Tips were rare and seldom significant. What I did receive in abundance was insults and unsolicited sexual suggestions from rude, spoiled college boys, and the girls who'd try to impress them by putting down the carhop, but I got free food!

Even more importantly, I had an excuse to get away from that tiny trailer and Momma, and I could play Steppenwolf's "Born to be Wild" over and over again on the jukebox. I only kept the job a few weeks though because walking the two miles down the highway in the heat of an Alabama summer was a hot, dusty and tiresome commute. I also figured out real quick-like that Momma would spend every penny I made as fast as I made it.

Chapter Nine - Splinter

California

Momma took a waitress job in Opelika and moved us out of the bubble trailer into a very old dilapidated house, an awful place, but big. Summer ended and school started up again, a time of year I always dreaded because I never did well academically. My average grade was "D" which I assumed meant– dumb. My childhood was confused and scattered at best, but I'm sure that moving every couple of months contributed to my inability to be a stellar student.

Shortly after we moved – I started yet another new school and made friends with a girl in my class that lived up the street. Glorianne had several brothers and sisters and lived in an old place very similar to our new digs. Whenever I'd go to her house and ask if she could come out to visit or walk to the store, she'd always make me wait five to ten minutes, it never occurred to me that this was odd.

One morning, very early, Glorianne knocked on our door to tell me she was leaving, that she was going to live with her real daddy. Her leaving seemed so out of the blue because she had never talked about moving or said she was unhappy. She never complained about her home life. I should have understood – I knew it didn't pay to complain – it only got you in trouble.

Glorianne looked so broken that morning. Her pretty young face awash with tears, trails of which ran down her face and neck. We sat down on the bare porch, still damp from the morning dew. She wept until she choked and then had to get past the hiccups of sorrow before she could tell me why she had to leave. Her stepfather had been forcing her to have sex with him before he'd allow her to go anywhere or for any other privilege. Glorianne left that same day and I never saw her again.

Two weeks after Glorianne moved away, I was sitting on the smelly couch that we inherited when we moved into the big house, its aged springs sticking me in the butt, watching Momma, half looped and in one of her moods. She was rolling a cigarette from a big blue can of Bugler tobacco. She rolled her own smokes when money was scarce, and it always was. Sitting cross-legged on the floor, she swayed back-and-forth, trying to sing – *Blues in the Night, My Mama done toll' me* – which she used to sing beautifully when I was a little girl, but her voice had been long gone for a long time.

Then she abruptly stopped the swaying and singing and eyeballed me with contempt for some real, or imagined problem or discomfort that I had caused her. She barked at me to toss her the rolling papers that were lying on the couch next to me. I did, never considering how much that one simple act would change my life. Two of the tiny papers broke loose from the package and sailed gently like little mini paper airplanes and landed on the floor a few feet away from Momma. She went berserk. You never knew what would set her off. She was an emotional time bomb, always tick, tick, ticking.

She screamed. "What in the hell is wrong with you, you clumsy little piece of shit?" Her verbal assault went on and on but this time, unlike the thousands of times before, I did not cry, hide, run, or beg. Not this time. Momma came after me, skittering across the floor like a spider on steroids. I screamed at her. "Leave me alone Momma, I ain't done nothin' to you." But she clawed at my face in a rage. What happened next shocked me as much as I am sure it floored Momma. I called on every ounce of courage I possessed, channeled my adrenaline, pulled my legs up to my chest, and kicked my momma clean across the room.

Not sure just what she might do next and not wanting to find out – I ran – not even thinking about where I might go. Eventually I found myself at the corner gas station standing in front of a phone booth, with an incredible idea forming in my mind. Maybe I could do what Glorianne had done, go live with my *real* daddy? I thought wow, what a crazy idea. I had no memory of ever seeing my daddy since he sent us away when I was two, and he had never once written or called me. You would think that and the fact that I did not know his phone number, should have deterred me. It did not.

With resolve, I stepped into the phone booth, closed the glass door, picked up the receiver, took a deep breath and inserted a trembling finger and dialed "O" for the operator. When the operator answered, I said, "I ain't got no number for him but I want to call my daddy."

I told her his name and that he lived in Half Moon Bay California. She said, "You hold on now, and I'll try to reach him for you," so I waited.

Time ticked intolerably slow, doubt began to fill my mind, a mind so strong just a minute before. Suddenly certain that the operator would tell me that she could not find the number. Or even worse, ask me to put money in the phone since I had none, she shocked me when she said, "Here y'all go, y'all have a nice day now."

And then a man's voice came on the line. "Hello, this is Carlo."

Holy shit. I couldn't believe it had worked! Excited and unsure of myself, I babbled, but when my daddy asked why I had called, I managed to say, "Momma's drunk and mean all the time, so can I come live with y'all?"

Daddy said little, and his silence made me ramble on in a nervous tirade of emotion in an attempt to make him understand, to hear me, to help me. Then I stopped rambling, I had to know. Would he want me? The silence stretched on and after what seemed an eternity, he finally said, "Hold on a minute, I'm going to let you talk to your step-mom."

This pattern would repeat itself over and over again throughout the coming years. He'd always pass me to his wife.

Lynda was very kind to me that day. She spoke with a quiet and gentle voice. I asked her if I could move to California and live with them, and to my surprise, she said yes. She told me that she had my grandparents' phone number, and would call them to arrange for me to be taken to the airport, as soon as she had booked a flight for me. Since I had no money to do so, I asked her to call my grandparents first before the airport and ask them to come and get me so I would not have to go back to Momma's.

After I returned the handset to the cradle, I stood frozen for a long time, peering out at the filth and poverty that permeated most areas I occupied as a child, from behind the dirty glass of an old phone booth. I couldn't believe it, I wanted to throw the door open wide and scream at the top of my lungs, I'm rescued, my daddy wants me and I'm going to California, me, Toni Pacini, me!

I did go back to Momma's house, but I waited for Grandpa in the front yard. She came out when Grandpa drove up, and I told her I was leaving for good, going to California. Although early in the day, she was already drunk, she gave me a dismissive, could-care-less wave of her arm, and went inside.

New Clothes and a Jet Plane

Everything happened so fast. Grandpa took me back to Momma's the next morning and while Momma slept off her latest binge, I packed the few things I owned, worth bothering to look for, in an old suitcase Grandma scrounged up somewhere for me. It was a small, ratty little blue thing, but it was my first suitcase. We always moved in cardboard boxes, croaker sacks, and paper bags, or tied it all up in sheets.

Later that same day, Grandma took me to J.C. Penney's and bought me a new outfit to wear on the airplane and a brand new pair of shoes. I had never had a new outfit from any place other than Woolworth's five-and-dime, and most of my new clothes were just new to me, hand-me-downs. Grandma got me a pale blue pantsuit with a pretty blouse. I felt like Mary Tyler Moore off to the big city.

The following day Grandpa paid Mr. Mobley, a neighbor, to drive me to the airport in Atlanta Georgia. Grandpa didn't drive that far anymore, and especially not in a big city like Atlanta. I found Atlanta overwhelming, the airport, and all the busy people. So completely overwhelming that I don't remember how I got on the plane and very little of the flight, but the landing was amazing and unforgettable.

There are no words to describe how I felt when the plane slowly descended below the fog and clouds, and the city of San Francisco came into view. Speechless, breathless, clueless, I pinched myself, not able to believe I may actually be awake and in California. Ten minutes later, I'm at the arrival gate, and there stood my daddy, a stranger to me. Christmas Eve 1968. Fourteen years old and out of the mill village.

My Daddy's House

My daddy's house would never be my home. Daddy and Lynda had a beautiful house on the coast south of San Francisco, near Lynda's parents. Lynda's children, John and Anne, spent a lot of their childhood days at their grandparents' home while Daddy and Lynda were busy building their dream house, having big parties, and going to local clubs their friends frequented or owned. Daddy did a great job of avoiding the kids, all of us. My sister Doreen, when she'd visit, always felt his resentment that she was in his home, his castle. John, Anne, and I, often felt the same.

Later, when my sister Deborah moved to California, she received more of the same from him. Daddy had a tricky, unpredictable temper, and we never knew what might upset him, so we stayed clear as much as possible. This was very emotionally confusing for me because I desperately wanted to be with him, to just sit near him on the couch, to take a walk together, damn...I'd have given my right arm to have him brush my hair or lovingly tuck me in at night. Instead, I'd stay in my room or sometimes linger in the bathroom to avoid running into him in the hall.

Regardless of my efforts to please him by being all but invisible, he was never pleased with me. Any contact was too much. Lynda did what she could to bridge the tremendous chasm between my daddy and me. She served as a good buffer between Daddy and her children, and she had her parents nearby to help, but she couldn't do anything to ease the pain I felt from my daddy's blatant rejection.

He was not that fantasy daddy I longed for all those lonely years. He proved to be nothing like that man.

The first time I saw Lynda was on Christmas Eve 1968, the afternoon Daddy picked me up at the San Francisco airport, and he and I drove silently to their home. They were having a huge Christmas party, and there were lots of people there. The rest of the evening is a blur. It's not easy to meet your daddy for the first time in the midst of a drunken shindig, and I had never seen such a huge modern home.

Daddy and Lynda's home was a fairy tale came to life, unreal, and it had an incredible ocean view. It was too beautiful to actually exist, I could not stop my eyes from hopping from one amazing site to another. Just when I thought it couldn't get stranger, I walked into a room that had a full bar and stained glass windows! It had a full bar right in the house! I had never seen a bar in a house before, only in Juke Joints, and stained glass windows were only in the fancy big city churches that had lots of money. I felt like I had just followed a rabbit down a freaky, freaky hole.

Old Baggage

Lynda cried when she saw the sad assortment of possessions I had brought from Alabama in my tiny beat-up little blue suitcase. When my grandpa took me to Momma's house to gather my belongings, I had found little worth taking. I'd packed a couple of worn-out outfits and some torn, stained underwear. I had no prized belongings, no baby blanket, and no photographs, no life to pack in a beat-up hand me down suitcase.

When Lynda saw what my case contained (or did not contain) compassion and maybe pity filled her eyes. I appreciated her concern but her emotional response to my reality left me more embarrassed than comforted. I realized for the first time just how ratty I must appear to people in the *real* world. The next day Lynda took me shopping for everything. Dresses and skirts, pretty blouses and pants, shoes, and new underwear. Although thrilled with the new clothes, walking through the huge mall and from one classy store to another, I felt like a leper in a Ms. America contest. To say I felt out of place would be paramount to calling an alligator a lizard.

Momma and I had only shopped at Woolworth's Five and Dime, or the musky basements in churches. Even the JC Penney's Grandma had taken me to for my airplane outfit was tiny and dull compared to the places Lynda took me to. Hillsdale Mall in San Mateo had sprawling fancy stores and huge escalators. It looked more like a museum with its cavernous ceilings and foliage in planters that were larger than some homes I had lived in. I felt conspicuous and awkward and I felt sure everyone was staring at me.

Daddy's Intolerance

Even before my visit to California in 1968 my sister Doreen, from Daddy's second marriage, would stay with Daddy and his family for a few days on occasion. Her visits always made things stressful for everyone, as Daddy would sulk and fume the entire time. My move to California amplified the stress. Then shortly after my arrival, my sister Deborah followed me from Alabama. I'd understand if Anne and John, my stepbrother and sister, were resentful of all of us newcomers. We didn't make their lives any easier. Our daddy was a difficult man before we showed up, but by the time we were all interacting in 1968-69, we had stretched Daddy's child-tolerance to the limit, especially since he had little or none to begin with.

Daddy has never been comfortable talking to people, but it has always been more troublesome for him to simply have a conversation with one of *his* children. Everything is a joke, mostly one-liners, often presented in the form of a question that he doesn't really want an answer to. When he'd see me in the hallway or when I'd walk into the kitchen and find him there, he'd say something like,

"Oh, it's you? So, you're still here?" Or, "How you do, Magoo?"

I never knew what to say to him. No matter how I responded to him, he'd just serve up another one liner, like, "How about that?" Then he'd quickly gather up his sliced sourdough and salami and leave the room. I always felt confused as to what I should do next.

Deborah

My sister Deborah followed me to California just in time for her sixteenth birthday. I arrived December twenty-fourth, and she followed in mid-February. Deborah and I had never coexisted in harmony, and that did not change when we moved to California. Almost as soon as her plane touched the tarmac, the arguments began.

A few months after Deborah arrived, Lynda and Daddy sat us down and said the situation had to change. I can remember the sinking feeling their words brought to me. I knew they did not want me. No one did. It wasn't just me; they didn't want either of us, but they could not be so direct as to pack both of us up and send us away. They said Deborah and I argued constantly and that it was hard on everyone in the home and especially difficult for John and Anne. The bottom line, one of us had to go back to Alabama.

Deborah started talking fast and made her case well. She pointed out the many ways that the arguing was my fault. She was good at pointing out my issues, my problems, and how it caused her to be upset and therefore argumentative. She had learned well from Momma how to blame others for her actions. Having never won a contest of will or word with Deborah; I gave up easily and went back to Momma. Daddy's house may have been beautiful but it was as lonely and empty as all of the holes Momma moved us into. The only thing that had changed was geography and I had fancy clothes.

110

Chapter Ten - The Wandering Years

Uprooted: 1969

The only address I can remember from my childhood, is 311 Twenty-Fourth Street, Opelika Alabama, my grandparents' little white house in Pepperell Mill Village. Until I started researching my family's history in preparation to write this book, I never thought about *before*, before. My mind only traveled short distances. There had been no time for *before* my time. No time before my birth, before the mill village, before I remembered. I never considered the fact that my grandparents had lived somewhere else before I existed.

My grandparent's house at 311 Twenty-fourth Street was the only certainty in my life. It was always there. It felt like my grandparents had always been there, and I suppose I thought they always would be. But in just the few months that I stayed with my daddy in California my grandparents did the unthinkable. They moved.

I couldn't believe it. I knew every inch of that old house, the holes in the screens that I got a switching for making with a pencil. The pattern left where the paint had peeled off the big pipe in the bathroom, the broken brick grate in the gas heater, my hiding place out back and the steps we played rock school on, the fig tree that Grandma made my favorite preserves from. When inside the house were anger and chaos, I found refuge in the tall grass in the back yard. I'd lie there and entertain my fantasies. My favorite was when my daddy would parachute out of a passing plane into the back yard and rescue me.

As a child the only way I had known my daddy was from the two photographs Momma carried of him. My favorite was of him in his uniform. Daddy had been a Paratrooper in the Army. But all I understood– when the grass waved tall and the earth felt cool on a hot day and when I needed to run away from things I could not change, was that he flew around in big airplanes and jumped out here and there as he pleased. From yellowed photographs and lonely childhood dreams, I wove this scene that I could play again and again, at will, my most precious special fantasy.

I'd hear the roar of the plane, and as it passed overhead, it would block out the sun, casting a huge, bird-like shadow over the back yard. I'd blink at this sudden change of light, and as I re-focused, I'd see a large figure falling rapidly through the cloudless sky, plummeting right toward me. Just as I was about to roll away to avoid being crushed –a beautiful parachute would unfurl like a huge colorful butterfly, yanking its load back up for a moment.

It appeared to have changed course, as if it were heading elsewhere instead of earth after all but setting off instead to explore the stars and the moon. It saddened me to see the beautiful butterfly pulling away, and thrilled me when I saw it start to gently descend again.

Closer and closer it came to where I sat, so all alone, and at last I'd squeal with uncontrollable delight when I realized that it was a man and not a butterfly at all. As I watched, the mysterious man glided gently to earth, the wind ruffling his pants legs, and landed with a thump about twenty feet away from me in the tall grass. He righted himself, removing his harness and then his headgear and to my astonishment, I realized it was my daddy, like an old photograph that comes to life.

We run open-armed to one another, that wild and awkward run of a child with arms flinging gracelessly to-and-fro. As the imaginary music swells like in the movies, he reaches me and picks me up, folding me into his big, strong arms, the arms of a hero, and he swings me round and round while we laugh and cry and laugh some more. Exhausted, we fall to our knees in the tall green grass, his large form towering over my tiny one. Then he tells me how he has been searching for me and that he loves me, and would never have left me but was forced to do so by my horrid mother.

Fantasy, my only escape. That familiar yard with its tall grass, my only sanctuary. No one could touch me there, in my mind. Now the place where I created my fantasies and that signified my only safety in a dangerous world was gone. There was no refuge, no home.

Tallassee, Alabama

My grandparents had moved to Tallassee where they had originally met and married. Grandma still had family there. So when they decided to move, and I never knew why they did, I suppose it was logical that they chose Tallassee. They had sold their house in Pepperell and bought a nice brick home, small but normal, on a nice street, and it wasn't in a mill village. So although I was once again the new kid in a new school, it wasn't as awful as in the past. One reason, I was from California (sort of) and I played it up. For the first time in my school career, other kids did not avoid me like a plague. I wasn't exactly popular, either, but it was better than I had ever expected. I'd failed a grade, so I was in the ninth grade and fifteen years old.

I met my first husband in Tallassee, Barry, a sweet, very tall, and gentle young man. I found it easy to fall in love with Barry because from the beginning I could tell he really saw me. I remember the first day I saw him. I was looking for my next class on my second day in Tallassee High School. I had walked the long halls for several minutes and had finally realized I was lost; at that moment a deep voice asked,

"Hey, you lost or something? Ain't you new here?" I looked up, way up, and found myself locked in an awkward stare with a sweet looking but not especially attractive young man. Neither of us seemed sure what to say or do next, and as the silence stretched out and filled the small space between us, I thought I might just turn tail

114

and run. Barry found his voice and again asked if I was new to the school, and I managed to answer him.

We were inseparable from that moment on. Barry seemed smitten with me. I had his rapt attention; more intense than any attention I had ever known. I did not find him attractive, but I'd been so hungry my whole life for attention, I could not resist him. Barry had an eight ball for a knob on the gearshift of his red impala. He was so cool! We'd park for hours at the lake and make out, drink, smoke pot, and listen to Jimi Hendrix and Janis Joplin on the eight-track.

Barry stood six feet two inches tall and skinny as a rail. He had a long, narrow face and a jaw that came to a sharp conclusion, like an exclamation point at the end of his face. But he was kind, decent, and intelligent, and he treated me with tender respect. He was well liked by the kids at our school and the faculty as well. I felt being with Barry lent credibility to me and gave me worth.

Barry had never been in any kind of trouble before he met me. I'm afraid I may not have been the best thing that ever happened to that good man. I suppose his time with me was an education, if not a blessing. I was fifteen when we married. I turned sixteen one month later, and Barry, barely eighteen. We did not choose to marry so young because of love, but because we wanted to be grownups. We wanted to party and come and go as we pleased, we wanted to have sex, and we wanted to make our own decisions. I wanted someone of my very own to protect and love me. We wanted to piss off his parents.

We did it for all the wrong reasons, but at the time it seemed like a great idea. I don't remember much of the wedding; I think we were both high on acid at the time. I have one photograph. I wore a knee-length white dress with poofy sleeves that came to my elbows. The bouquet was small but pretty. Both Barry and I looked terrified. It's not a photograph to be framed. For our honeymoon, we stayed in a tiny cabin at a local lake for a couple of days. The place was decrepit and infested with a large variety of insects and aggressive roaches. After our honeymoon, we rented a dark, damp basement apartment in Tallassee with no windows, and the insanity really began.

Somewhere along the way we met a hustler, a card shark con man named Ace. Too classic, eh? He lived with us on and off, and we partied around the clock. After a few crazy months of June and Ward on Fantasy Island, Barry's parents and our neighbors made it clear that our lifestyle was not acceptable in God fearin' Alabama. Barry's mother and father were highly respected in Tallassee. They had the picture-perfect, rambling brick home with a long, winding driveway that led up to the house from the old country road that meandered lazily past. They were middle class, devout and rigid Christians, and terribly concerned about how they looked and what the neighbors might think or say. They had not been happy when Barry married so below them and so young. They finally laid down the law, their law, "Straighten up or get out; you both are an embarrassment to us."

A few days later we loaded some clothes and our eight-track tapes into Barry's red Impala and set out for California. I had no idea that morning how many times I'd make that trip. We drove old Route 66 with all of its fruit stands, Indian trading posts, and roadside oddities. We picked up hitchhikers, smoked dope, ate bologna sandwiches on white bread out of a dirty foam ice chest, and danced on the side of the road to the blaring tunes from the car's eight-track system.

We slept at rest stops or state parks and spooned together under the night sky in our sleeping bag. We stopped at most of the roadside come-ons. We checked out giant snakes, arrowheads, meteorites, and lots of ice cream and other munchies. Old Route 66, was a hippie's Disneyland.

Berkeley, California

Our little cross country roller coaster ride ended up in Berkeley where we made friends with a group of long haired hippies in tie-dyed T-shirts, beads, and multi-patched bell-bottom jeans. Our new friends were more than happy to share our pot and in return they were generous with their Red Mountain wine poured from a gallon jug with a screw cap. The walls of their apartment were covered with rugs and colorful bed spreads. A beaded curtain hung in the doorway between the living room and kitchen.

On every coffee table in the city of Berkeley, laid a worn copy of "Be here now" by Ram Dass. I remember thinking to myself, "where else would I be now if not where I am?" Some parts of the movement eluded me, but nonetheless Barry and I were very impressed with Berkeley. After all the party was the main reason we had gone to California in the first place.

Berkeley, a university town, had a huge pool of eligible cheap labor, with students available to work part-time, so that meant Barry and I had no success with attempts to find work. We spare changed for a while for the Berkeley Free Clinic. The clinic supplied a can with a lock on it, and we'd hang out on Telegraph Avenue and solicit donations. We were given a portion of what we collected at the end of the day.

We often ate free lunch at the Hare Krishna temple or the local soup kitchen. Eventually, Barry sold his beloved red Impala, and when that money ran out and we could no longer party, we hitchhiked back to Alabama with our tails between our legs.

We moved in with Barry's older sister in Tallassee, and Barry enlisted in the Army. That was the only way to satisfy his parents that he was seriously going to straighten up. I promised to wait faithfully for him at his sister's until he sent for me, but less than a month later I moved on. I returned to Opelika where I flopped on the couches of new friends I made along the way until I answered an ad in the local newspaper and ended up back on the road to California, again.

Chapter Eleven - Accruing Scars

Stripped Bark

I answered an ad in the Auburn newspaper posted by a young man, Michael, who was looking for a companion to share the driving and gas with him on a road trip to California. I could not drive and I did not have any money, but the guy thought I was cute and let me come along anyway. That is how I ended up back in Berkeley in early 1971.

When we arrived in Berkeley, I looked up a young man, Randy, that I had met when Barry and I had visited a few months before, and he allowed Michael and I to crash at his place. Once again I looked for work, but I had no real skills, and there were plenty of eager young laborers in Berkeley. Finally, in desperation, I answered an ad for Nude Models.

At the interview I had mixed emotions when the manager actually hired me. Glad to have a job, and yet terrified to do the job. I returned the following day with butterflies the size of condors in my stomach. It worked like this: We, the other models and myself, would go into a dressing room, undress, put our clothes in a locker and cover ourselves with a sheet.

The clients who were mostly legitimate art students would walk through and choose an individual whose look met their specific needs. The agency was a respectable place, with no hanky-panky or side business going on. It was near the Berkeley campus, and they did a great business with the local art students, individually and as groups.

I experienced a confusing array of emotions. I felt terrified that someone would choose me, and yet afraid they would not. I needed the job. However, I did not want to pose naked in front of a stranger, not at any price. The oddest emotion of all was the need I had to be chosen. I needed to validate that I was actually visible, like the unpopular child on the playground, while the most popular kids, who were always the team captains, were choosing sides for a game.

If you were not chosen until last, you had not really been chosen at all, but simply accepted due to a lack of choice on the part of the last captain. You might hate the captains, and you might not even want to play the silly game. You could be asthmatic and unable to play, but you *must* be chosen.

To my delight and horror, a young man chose me. I followed him to the studio he had reserved and posed in the manner he requested. The session was only half an hour, maybe forty-five minutes, and the young artist was nothing but respectful and business-like. My stomach in knots, my palms sweaty, and my heart pounding in my chest. I fought the urge to run, taking each moment, each breath, one at a time.

Afterward, I went to my locker, dressed quickly and scooted out the door before anyone even noticed that I'd left. I never went back or asked for my pay. I couldn't do that over and over again. I only stayed in California a short time but before I left I adopted a black Irish setter puppy from a girl on Telegraph Avenue.

I named the little squiggly-wiggly pup "Canna" after cannabis sativa. Then Ms. Canna and I set out hitchhiking across country. My sister Deborah had recently moved to Yonkers, New York, with a new boyfriend. I hoped they'd let me stay a while, but that door would not be open when I knocked on it after a long journey across America. She gave no reason when she coldly said, "No," So I went on to Albany, New York. I'm not sure why I made the decision to go to Albany, but off I went, these were my wandering years.

Albany, New York

I arrived in Albany on a cold, rain-soaked night. A group of teenagers hanging out in a small park directed me to a local youth hostel where I crashed for several weeks. I met Dana Black the first night there. He worked as a volunteer counselor at the hostel. Dana tried to help me, he was a good counselor, but by the time I drifted into that facility, I had been severely bent and twisted for far too long. I stayed several weeks but as was the norm for me, surrounded by people, I felt totally alone. So before the worst part of the winter season arrived in Albany, I packed my backpack and tied an old rope on my dog and headed back to Alabama.

I hitched a ride with a van full of hippies who were headed down to Florida. They agreed to take me as far as Statesboro, Georgia. I had $26.00 to get me home – so to be careful – I stashed a $20.00 bill in a tiny box with a rubber band wrapped around it several times, and then further concealed it in the center of my clothing in my backpack. I only allowed myself to spend the additional $6.00 I had, from Albany down to Georgia.

On a nippy morning, the driver of the van dropped me off at a four-way intersection in front of a restaurant, just inside Statesboro city limits. It'd been a long time since I'd had a hot meal. I'd eaten peanut butter and crackers from my backpack for the most part the past couple of days, other than handouts from the other passengers in the van. Only having two hundred more miles to go, I figured that with minimal luck I'd be home by nightfall so I gave myself permission to break my last twenty.

I enjoyed a big breakfast and saved scraps of bacon, biscuit, and egg for Canna. When the waitress brought the check, I pawed through my backpack for my money and freaked when I couldn't find it. Panicked, I pulled out everything and piled it onto the cheap vinyl seat next to me in the booth. I found it. Whew. My heart slowed, but when I opened the box it was empty. Unwillingly, I started to cry. So tired, alone, and scared. What the hell would happen to me now?

The waitress came over, clearly concerned for me and I explained what had happened and begged her to believe me. I was pleasantly surprised by her kindness, as I had very little experience with kindness from strangers. Most people would look the other way at best and be downright vicious at worst.

She told me not to worry about it. I insisted on her name and address and promised to send her the money as soon as I could. I left there with renewed hope for mankind, although disgusted with my fellow passengers in the van, one of which had clearly robbed me while I slept or peed. I had no way of knowing how little hope I'd have left for mankind before the day was over. I went off in sweet innocence to finish my journey.

Canna and I stood on the wide, gravelly shoulder of the highway in front of the restaurant, and I put out my thumb. There was very little traffic, so we'd been there for a good while before a car stopped just up the road from us. I immediately noticed there were two men in the car and made a decision to turn down the ride. I had a policy to never get into a car with more than one man and preferred a car with a woman in it.

Canna was off the rope, playing in the open field beside the road while we waited for cars. She knew the hitchhiking procedure. You wait, car stops, get in, car stops, get out, you wait, car stops, get in. As soon as the car stopped up the road from us, Canna ran to it. I quickly gathered our things and started toward the parked car to tell them no thanks. My heart sank when the man in the passenger seat reached over the back seat and opened the back door and to my horror, Canna jumped right in. I ran then, calling "Canna!"

When I got to the car, I told her to get out, but she sat there wagging her tail, oblivious to the possible danger. The man on the passenger side of the car got out, and both men were saying,

"Oh, come on girl. Get in, we'll give you a ride, you don't have nothin' to be afraid of from us; we're just a couple of good-o-boys."

It felt like a bad dream. My gut said "Nooooo!" All I had for protection was my intuition, and the red flags were flying, but as I tried to get Canna out, the men coaxed me in. One man picked up my backpack from where I had dropped it on the ground and put it in the back floorboard. Everything was moving fast and out of control, I am not certain exactly what happened – I think the man pushed me into the car. Nonetheless, there I sat – Canna gleefully wagging her tail – and me hoping that they really were good-o-boys.

They were not. We drove for a couple of miles and all the while the two strangers in the front seat drank from a bottle of Southern Comfort. When I refused to join them in a drink, the trouble began. One of the men accused me of not wanting to drink out of their bottle because they were black. I said, "That's not true, I just don't want any."

But the die was cast. This gave them the excuse they needed, not that they needed one, to do whatever they chose. When I realized the direction the tide was turning, I tried to soothe the situation by patronizing them. I even took a drink from the bottle. Then the man driving turned onto a side road; he said he had to pee.

He drove up the logging road for an eighth of a mile or so and parked in a small turnout surrounded by pine trees. He got out of the car and took a few steps into the woods to do his business.

That's when the man in the passenger seat reached over and started touching me. He suggested I get into the front seat. I said no, and he reached for me. I fought and tried to open the car door, but the driver was there, at my door. I'd been so damned busy trying to fight off the man in the front seat that I hadn't noticed the other man return to the car.

Canna started to whine, and then growl, and got in the middle of it. The man on the outside of the car reached in, through the now-open car door, grabbed Canna by the collar and the hair on her back, and threw her into the woods. I heard her scream in pain, but I couldn't see her, I couldn't help her, I couldn't help myself.

The man in the car with me scrambled over the front seat. I flailed at him without effect, and he punched me several times. I was determined to make things difficult for them, but as the driver crawled back into the front seat, he turned, showing me a large knife and said,

"If you don't stop fighting us, I'll skin that damned dog of yours alive while you watch."

I went limp. I knew I had no hope of sparing myself whatever pain they chose to inflict, but maybe I could save Canna. I made myself be still and as invisible as I could. I couldn't control the tears or the vomit, but I kept my eyes closed and went as far away as

I could, deep, deep into places in my mind that I had never visited before. Then it was over. No, it will never be over. But the men stopped brutalizing me and threw me out of the car like a bag of garbage, tossing my clothes and my backpack after me. I sat half-naked in the dirt and watched as they sped off, throwing up a huge red cloud of Georgia red clay dust in their wake.

Slowly, reluctantly, I returned to my bruised and aching body. I managed to find my legs, then my arms, and then my clothes. After I pulled my jeans on, I went into the woods in the direction the man had thrown Canna, my heart breaking, fearing what I might find. My beautiful loving baby, broken. I found her cowering in the brush but alive.

The terror in her eyes acted as a mirror to reflect my own. I wanted to join her crouched beneath the brush, but I knew we had better get out of there before they changed their minds and came back to kill us, or worse. We made our way to the main road and walked back toward town. I was watching every direction and decided that if I saw a car coming, I would not take the chance that it might not be them; I would hide. I knew I had to get to a house to ask for help, to call the police.

After walking at least three miles with Canna noticeably limping, I saw a house off the road, a-ways down in the woods. I thought of the kind waitress and hope sprang forth that there were nice people in this town, not just monsters. I needed to believe I'd find compassion and much needed assistance. We took the dirt road to a path that led to the house made of small plank boards that looked like it had been planted in that place, long before the large grove of Loblolly pines that surrounded it arrived, to offer shade. If it had ever been painted, the color had faded long ago.

The place stood quiet, too quiet, dark and dwarfed by the forest. There were spots between the towering giants where the rays of the sun broke through the green leaf ceiling, and they tried to cheer the place, but to no avail. I cautiously approached the old structure and climbed the wobbly steps that led to the porch, on legs just as unstable. I knocked and waited, silence the only answer. I knocked again and a woman's voice said through the closed door, laced with suspicion,

"Who are you and what do you want?"

Relieved someone was home and especially grateful it was a woman, I asked her through the closed door to please call the police for me. I told her that two men had hurt me, and I feared that they might come back after me. She said she'd call the police, but that she did not want me on her porch and told me to wait in the yard.

Grateful she was making the call, I dared not ask for more, so I left the porch and waited for the police in the unseen woman's front yard. Having no choice, I sat down on the ground and held tight to Canna, amazed that she didn't have a broken leg or worse, but other than a limp and the fear in her beautiful brown eyes, she seemed to be okay.

Finally, a police car pulled into the driveway. I rushed to the vehicle, to the two officers who made no effort to get out of the car. I described my abusers and the car they were driving as best I could and asked the officers to go get them, grateful to finally have some help and protection. That's not the way the policemen saw it.

They arrested me for hitchhiking and took Canna and me to jail. They made crude jokes and directed snide remarks toward me all the way to the jailhouse. I was concerned they might also rape me once we got there. They said I deserved what I got, that a girl hitchhiking alone had all but asked to be raped. But when we got to the jail, they put me in a cell and locked Canna inside with me. I felt so grateful that they allowed her to stay with me. At least we had each other for comfort and warmth. The next morning, they dropped me off at the city limits and drove away after giving me a good talking to about living a Christian life.

I still do not understand how those men can live with themselves, the two men who raped me, or the cops who refused to help. I also would not want to be that frightened old woman in the woods for even a minute. I am still grateful to the waitress for her kindness. Kindness is rare, but maybe it's because true kindness comes so seldom that it is so sweet.

Auburn, Alabama

I made it to Alabama that day without further incident, no more robberies or rapes. Of course, I never told anyone what had happened to me in Statesboro. What good would that do? Swallow the soap and never tell.

I took a waitress job at a restaurant in Auburn called the Copper Kettle. The Kettle had been in Auburn for many years and was considered a landmark. I ate most of my meals at the restaurant, and I'd also take food home for Canna and me. It was a good deal. A day with food was always a good day.

When I first got into town, I stayed with Momma for a couple of weeks until I rented a room in Auburn at an old motel. The motel had not operated as a motel for a long time and there had been little maintenance given to the place. The rooms were barely habitable but cheap. Lots of young people, mostly stoners, not students, were renting the rooms. There were no kitchens, but we all had hot plates and shared a refrigerator in a community room that had once been the office.

I quickly learned that putting food in the fridge and expecting to find it there later was naïve, so I bought a $2.00 ice chest that I kept in my room and brought home ice from the Copper Kettle daily. One afternoon, while hanging out in a neighbor's room with several other tenants, smoking a joint, we were startled out of our drug-induced stupor by a blood-curdling scream.

We ran outside to find Canna lying on the side of the road where a logging truck had just hit her. The truck kept going. I held her bleeding head in my lap while she drew her last breath. I saved her in Statesboro from the rapist, but I couldn't keep her safe from everyday traffic. I couldn't keep myself safe. With my life a mess and Canna gone, I was alone again.

Chapter Twelve - Flicker of Hope

No Prince for Me

He came into my life like most things did, ripping and tearing and draped in shadow. Ben worked as a surveyor on a construction crew working temporarily in Auburn. He lived in an old hotel next to the restaurant where I worked, the Copper Kettle. The hotel rooms did not have kitchens, so he ate most of his meals at the restaurant. We had only dated for a few weeks when I became concerned about our relationship because Ben seemed to be more possessive, controlling, and unpredictable with each passing day.

When I served his chicken fried steak to him at the Copper Kettle's counter – the first day we met – he brought me to life with his attention. Ben was handsome, employed, and breathing, everything I wanted in a man, and most of all he really seemed to like me. But too soon he started with the possessive controlling behavior that I knew so well, I soon feared him as much as I desired him.

He'd slam me against the wall, accuse me of seeing other men, and having sex with my boss. His love had made me feel visible, but his rage made me disappear again. We'd dated for three months when I missed my period. Terrified I went to the clinic and confirmed that I was six weeks pregnant. My first instinct was to run, and only having my instincts to depend on, I listened to my gut and ran. The writing was already on the wall – Ben had been abusive and controlling, and I knew I'd never get away from him if he found out about the baby.

So at seventeen, pregnant and alone, I once again left Alabama, hitchhiking. I returned to Albany, New York, with the idea that I'd find a job, a place to live, and have my baby. He or she and I would be a family, and we'd be a perfect example of a happy-ever-after. Oh yeah...denial is the best drug ever, but not always the cheapest.

Camelot/Nikusake

Back in New York, I took jobs at two different fast food restaurants. It was late June, and I knew I had to get everything in place for the baby fast before winter came with the snow I dreaded. I scrambled frantically for a few weeks, but finally I admitted to myself that I was not making enough money for me to survive alone, much less with a baby.

Reluctantly, I left the safety of the womb of denial and entered the realm of reality once again. I have never liked it there. Reality is over-rated. I barely made enough money to pay my rent so I realized, reluctantly, that I had to find a better job and an adoption agency for my child. I found the new job within two weeks but the adoption agency did not come so easily.

I landed a good job at the Camelot/Nikusake Restaurant, once again working as a waitress. It paid much better than the places I usually worked for and the tips were incredible. The Camelot/Nikusake was actually two restaurants that shared one entrance in the same building. The Camelot, where I served, was an upscale dinner house that served prime rib, filet mignon, beef Wellington, and fine wine. The restaurant, furnished with dark paneling, engraved woods, plush antique carpets, and bright eloquent lighting, was magnificent.

I worked at the Camelot until I was almost seven months pregnant and showing too much to look appropriate in my uniform, at which time my boss offered me the job of evening hatcheck girl. As the hatcheck girl, I sat behind a small counter taking coats, hats, scarves, and gloves in exchange for a small tag with an identification number printed on it. It was boring, but I still had a paycheck.

A distinguished elderly gentleman, who dined at the Camelot almost every night and had apparently done so for many years, took an interest in me. An interest that I did not understand at the time. I had waited on him a few times when I worked as a waitress, but I had never really talked to him about anything, other than his dinner choice. He always sat at the same table and everyone knew him and treated him with utmost respect. The gentleman was always polite, but he never seemed to really see me; after all, it was my job and my nature to be invisible while of service.

After I took the job as the evening hatcheck girl, the old man seemed to notice me for the first time. No male had ever shown me the least bit of attention for anything other than sex, but this elderly man did not look at me in *that* way. He'd ask if I wasn't bored just sitting there all evening and inquire as to why I did not read a book to occupy my time.

I found his concern touching but thought his ideas were silly. Reading was a waste of time, and besides, nothing could be as interesting as the people, the fancy, seemingly normal people with lives, coming and going, spending more money on one dinner party than I made in three weeks. Was there?

One night the old man brought me a book and suggested I read a short story from it, a story that remains to this day one of my favorites. The book, a collection of poems and short stories by Edgar Allan Poe, was huge and felt too big, too heavy for my hands, too heavy for my mind. Nonetheless, the gentleman left it in my care and suggested I read "Hop-Frog," which also is known as "The eight chained ourang-outangs," and said he'd talk to me about it the following evening.

I did not want to read the damned story but I didn't want him to ask me about it later and have to admit I hadn't read it. Besides, there might be a nice tip in it for me. That night I did read "Hop-Frog" just to be able to say I had, or so I intended, but to my complete surprise, I loved it. I not only read Hop-Frog but several poems as well; by morning I was hooked. That evening, the gentleman did something no one had ever done before; he asked MY opinion, and he discussed the story with me. He seemed genuinely interested in what I thought of it and whether or not I had enjoyed reading it.

Wow. There are no words to express what that one wonderful man did for me that night in a hatcheck booth. He continued to bring me books and discuss them with me. He brought several of the classics, including works by Henry David Thoreau and Emerson. I owe him a huge debt and give him my greatest gratitude. He gave me an appreciation for my own mind, my brain, my worth, my ability to read and comprehend, and he opened doors to people, places, things, feelings, opinions, and concepts I had never imagined!

He did not mention the fact that I was quite obviously pregnant. He never asked about my Southern accent, where I lived, or why I wasn't in my senior year at some high school preparing for graduation and the prom. I sincerely believe he saved my life, and I don't even remember his name. I feel sure, however, that he would have said,

"Don't worry about my name -just keep reading."

Thank you kind sir, I will.

Lost

I struggle to remember the names of people, places, and things, but I easily remember the feelings, the smells, and the fear or the peace the moment held for me. Our minds have little built-in camcorders. We need no photograph, no special album in which to store scraps of Kodak paper, it's all burnt into our minds, etched deep in our souls, to view again and again, sometimes bidden, sometimes not.

At six-and-a-half months' pregnant, I looked and felt huge. Scared and desperately lonely, I'd often sit on the front stoop of my apartment, when it was warm, to pass the time. I hadn't made any progress with the adoption agencies. I had called and visited several but I left each one unimpressed. They all seemed to care more about the religious beliefs of the adoptive parents and the future indoctrination of my child, than his happiness and development.

I knew I had nothing to give my baby, but I wanted him to have a shot at happiness, a chance to be loved, which would be more than I ever had. I did not want him to be forced into multiple baptisms in order to please others' fanaticism. My childhood experiences – still so fresh in my memory as I was still a child – had given me a bad taste for forced religion. The God I believed in at seventeen required no rituals or dog and pony shows. I believed that we were all loved by our Creator, whatever we chose to call him or her, simply because we were their creation.

So displeased with the narrowness of the agencies I encountered, I continued to search for the right choice. I didn't want my baby's religious beliefs to be predetermined by an agency or

136

anyone, and I did not like the cold and institutional approach the places I visited offered. No place felt safe or welcoming.

As time passed, and with my due date fast approaching, my anxiety mounted. I was not a model mother, not even while carrying my child, and I knew I could not care for a dependent child. When I wasn't at the restaurant, I lived on a diet of Triscuit crackers and cream cheese. Lonely, afraid, uneducated, and poor as dirt, I did not want to do to my child what my parents had done to me.

Momma was not parented. As a young girl her parents made her quit school and take care of her two brothers. Daddy's mom ran away when he was a baby leaving him to be raised in orphanages and temporary homes. Neither one qualified to be parents, nor did either of them *want* to be parents, yet I was born, continuing the chain. No, I decided then and there to break that stubborn yolk of dysfunction. I vowed to never have another child. I'd find a home for the baby I carried and he'd be my last.

I kicked myself daily for not having had an abortion early on. Of course, at almost seven months along there was no choice short of suicide, an option I considered more than once. So I sat on the stoop, worked as long as I could, applied for welfare and county medical to pay for the birth, and waited alone in terror for whatever would come to pass. Powerless to change the course already set in place.

One lonely day, as I sat on the stoop, a man who I watched walk by occasionally, to my surprise, stopped to say hello to me. A young-looking older man who carried himself as if he didn't have a care in the world, well dressed but casual, polite but distracted, as if he was thinking of a dozen important things, all at once. In the past when I watched him walk by, certain he had not even noticed me sitting there, less than six feet away, I wondered what he might be thinking.

Pleased that he stopped to talk to me, delighted for a moment's notice, I found him pleasant and attentive. I enjoyed talking to him. He continued to stop on a regular basis after that, just to check on me. I had no idea why he seemed to care, but even the passing interest of a stranger comforted me, salved my lonely heart. Through little bites of information, gleaned from our conversations, I understood that he had something to do with a local university, I didn't know what exactly; I assumed he might be a teacher.

One day he said he had something serious to discuss with me, that he knew a couple from Tennessee that might be interested in adopting my baby. The couple was in Syracuse while the woman was attending school, studying to become a psychologist or a therapist of some sort. Her husband already had a degree in psychology and upon completion of the wife's studies they intended to return to Tennessee to live and work. They were actively trying to adopt and were very interested when they were told about my situation.

I consented to talk to them, I wanted to meet them in person but it was not allowed. We spoke over the phone. Once I agreed to give them my child, after several long probing conversations, they had a telephone put in my apartment so they could check on me, and assure that I could call a cab when I needed to go to the hospital. They hired an attorney and I met with him twice. Everything was on paper. Pages and pages and pages of paper, and I signed, and signed, and signed my name. This would have been the beginning of September 1972, barely eighteen, a baby myself, yet all grown up.

November 2, 1972

Five in the morning, I woke terrified, something felt terribly wrong. My bed and nightgown were soaked as if someone had dumped a bucket of water on me. I had no idea what to expect from labor, but I never imagined this. What the hell was all this wetness? It wasn't blood. Had a pipe broken in the ceiling above my bed? When I realized the liquid had come from my body, I knew it had to be bad news. I got dressed and called a cab to go to the hospital, certain I had lost my baby.

Apparently I am one of the lucky ones. My labor lasted less than three hours, and my son arrived just before eight am. Although brief in comparison to most women's labor, I still could not believe the pain. I am grateful no one had told me how unbearably awful it would be, or I'd have been even more frightened than I already was. Sometimes ignorance really is bliss.

As soon as they put me in a bed, I begged for something to block the pain. The nurses quickly became irritated with me, because they insisted my labor had just begun. They said I would not be ready for pain medication for several hours. When I insisted the baby was coming, an especially nasty nurse said, "Girl, you didn't even know that your water had broke; now you think you know when the baby is coming?"

She's lucky I couldn't get to my feet, or I'd have been on her like a flea on a hound dog; she should know better than to mess with a crazy woman in labor!

I eventually caused such a ruckus that a doctor reluctantly came in to check on me. He chastised me for being such a bother while he examined me. I took a moment's pleasure from his obvious shock when he admitted that my son was indeed on his way. They rushed me into the delivery room just in time.

I chose not to see my son. I knew seeing him would make letting go even harder. The next two days I focused on my pain, emotional and physical, and tried not to think of the son that I'd created but would never see. On the third day, I got up and dressed to go home. I thought the nightmare was almost over – and like so many other times of horror in my life – I'd deal and heal and move on. Eventually it would all be a fuzzy memory that I'd avoid when possible, and drown in food, drugs, booze, or sex when I could not.

The attorney had arranged it all; a third party hired by his office would pick up my son at the hospital and take him to his new parents. As far as I knew, my part was over except for the final papers that I'd sign in two weeks. But you know what they say about planning the results. Packed and eager to leave, I freaked when a nurse entered my room with my baby in her arms. I violently threw words at her, "What in the hell are you doing? I can't see him; why did you bring him here?"

The nurse explained that the hospital could not release my baby to the woman in the lobby – sent by the attorney's office – it was against hospital policy. If I later changed my mind about giving my son away, I could sue the hospital. This made sense, of course, but I didn't care; I couldn't do it. I couldn't carry my baby downstairs cradled in my arms and then hand him to a stranger. Damn all the Gods, I was not supposed to have to do that.

In the end – like always – I did what I had to do. They put me in a wheelchair and placed my son in my trembling arms. I tried not to look, I told myself – just hold on, this will all be over in a couple of minutes – it's just an elevator ride, just hold on, and don't look.

Then something gently touched my chin and I couldn't help it, I looked. I looked deep into the dark, beautiful eyes of my baby boy, my son. He had reached up with his tiny hand and touched my chin with his perfect fingers, and I looked, damn it! I looked.

My Son's Face

Thick, dark hair – big bottomless eyes – he was breathtaking, and I gave him my breath freely, along with my heart. For a few minutes I knew love – I knew him –and then he was gone.

The elevator doors opened, and we rolled into the lobby and out through the double glass doors into the day. A woman waited there. Nondescript – just a woman – and she took him. I let her. I sat there and just let her take him from my arms and walk away, forever.

Calmly I stood and walked back into the lobby, carrying my small overnight bag. My womb was not the only part of me left empty, I felt colder and emptier than I had ever felt before. I walked over to the phone on the information desk – the one connected directly to the local cab company – I lifted the receiver. There was a ring or two and a dispatcher answered. I opened my mouth to request a cab, but all that came out was a deep guttural scream. I screamed and cried, wailed and moaned. I couldn't swallow the soap this time. It stuck in my throat. People stared and stepped around me, whispering to one another. I heaved and whimpered until I drained my heart enough to regain control.

Then I called a cab and went home, alone. I thought I had known lonely; I had not. I still see him. I still feel him in my arms. I still smell him. I still love him. I still miss him.

Escape

Until that day, the day I gave a stranger my son, I drank and used other drugs just to feel better, to fit in, to loosen up, to forget, to help me pretend. From that day forward and for the next fourteen years, I drank to die, too much of a coward to kill myself and too afraid to live. I chose slow suicide through the bottle, with its lovely, numbing effect and sweet oblivion. I had little hope before, just a tiny flicker, but on that day on a sidewalk in front of a hospital in Albany New York, that fragile flicker went out, and I walked a long time in total darkness.

Darkness to me is not about Satan or demons. It is about hopelessness. Where there is no hope, there is no light. Without hope there is no reason for tomorrow. I had no reason. Two weeks after I left the hospital, I went to the attorney's office to sign the final papers. The huge, classy office building made me feel small and conspicuous. I always felt like illiterate white trash in such places, and that day was worse than most because I knew, they knew, that I had given my baby away.

After I signed the papers, the attorney took the elevator down with me. The building was in downtown Albany and sat on the corner of two main streets; there were lobby doors available from either street, and the lobby was huge. I had told the attorney more than once – as usual nervously rambling – that I'd have named my son Joshua if I had kept him. I suppose I just needed to be heard.

Anyway, we said farewell in the lobby, and he headed one way out one set of doors, and me the other, but before he walked away, I asked him one thing. I asked him to please tell me my son's first name. I knew he couldn't tell me the last name, but I really felt a need to put a name to my child's memory. The attorney was kind and apologized, but insisted he could not tell me. I walked away. Then, as I pushed the heavy glass lobby door, he called my name. I turned and he said one word:

"Joshua." and he turned and walked out of the door.

I've always thought that he was most likely just being kind, that my son's adoptive parents had not really named him Joshua. But it pleased me nonetheless. He will always be Joshua to me.

Afterbirth

Two weeks after I gave birth to Joshua, I returned to work at the Camelot, where I resumed my original position as a waitress, no longer the hatcheck girl. Pleased to have the big tips back, I nonetheless found I missed the solitude of the hatcheck room where, thanks to a wonderful man, I had spent hours consuming mass quantities of words.

Two days back on the floor as a waitress, I started to hemorrhage. The doctor said I had returned to work too soon, and I tried to lay low, but as usual I needed money. I did eventually heal, and within six weeks I went back to work full-time. My son had been born the first week of November 1972. It's damned cold in New York that time of year. I wanted out.

I considered heading back to Alabama, but I didn't dare hitchhike in the winter. Having been stuck out in the snow a couple of times when hitchhiking, I dared not leave until spring. So I stayed in Albany, working at the Camelot/Nikusake, and waited out the winter. As soon as the snow started to melt and the temperatures became bearable, I took off once again, always in the wind.

Chapter Thirteen - Wild Willie

The Drug Dealer-1973

I had lived with him for almost a year when he told me that he had noticed me walking the sidewalks in the mill village since I was a young girl. He said he'd been attracted to me even then. Later, after therapy and a little maturity, I realized how twisted that made him. He worked as a truck driver for the mill and drove through the village on weekdays. He admitted watching me from the time I was as young as eight years old.

I would have been barely in my teens when the mill fired him. He said his bosses were out to get him, but I'm sure his ill temper and drug addiction were a big part of his dismissal. Willie didn't live near the mill so once he was fired; he no longer drove through the village daily.

Certain that I was invisible, I wondered how he had seen me? Had he silently observed me as I purposely stepped on every crack in the sidewalk? Other kids would avoid the cracks, jumping from one spot to the other on one foot like they were playing hopscotch while they chanted, *Step on a crack and break your Momma's back.* But, sometimes, when alone, I'd step on all of them. I stomped them as hard as I could. I had so much unexpressed anger; I released it with my small secret rebellions.

146

Having just returned to Alabama from New York, a month before my nineteenth birthday, I met some kids in a bar. They invited me to a party. We drove quite a ways and ended up at an old house out in the country, well off the beaten path.

Out of the car, my new friends grabbed several empty paper bags and headed across the road. I followed, although apprehensive. I noticed that there were other people in the field and they appeared to be having a great time. So when the boy in front of me grabbed the top piece of barbed wire and pulled it up, while pushing the bottom piece down with his boot, creating a hole for me to step through, I did. I thought, "What the hell – I've been to stranger places."

So, the first time I saw Wild Willie, he was gathering Psilocybin mushrooms, plucking them one by one, like picking daisy's, from the cow shit they love to grow in.

He seemed to completely ignore me, but I couldn't stop looking at him. He had long white hair that hung past his shoulders and a white beard. I thought he looked like Willie Nelson. Definitely way too skinny, but his eyes were inviting, and what attracted me most of all, he was in control, totally in control.

Our bags filled, we returned to Willie's house where we boiled down the mushrooms and made a dark, murky brew. We cut it with Lipton's sweetened iced tea, because by itself, it tasted disgusting. Psilocybin mushrooms are in the hallucinogenic family of recreational drugs.

They take you to a magic place, a place that tells your logical self that all is well and groovy, even when it's not. I had used mushrooms before that night – but that evening the high freed me from past fears and inhibitions and left me feeling potent. I basked in a sense of well-being and power that I had never known. An illusion, yes, but the experience made me larger and more visible than I had ever been. Until it did not.

We drank our magic potion and a lot of beer that afternoon. Willie had cases of cold cans of Pabst Blue Ribbon. Understandably, much of the night that followed was a blur. At some point, he and I started talking, and we stayed awake all night wired on drugs. I rarely left his side for two years from that day.

A couple of years older than my daddy, forty-seven, Willie was twenty-eight years older than me. A guru to the kids, he had drugs, money and booze, a house, cars, a truck, and several motorcycles. He spelled security for me and I desperately longed for security, if only for a short respite. It'd been my life's story to be discounted and ignored by adults, my parents included, and it was therefore always the case that any adult who paid special attention to me turned my head.

You want to chase your child into the arms of an adult predator? Ignore them. Make them feel invisible. Then all a predator has to do is pay a little attention. No candy or puppies required.

I cannot say that I loved him, but I had never been anyone's priority before. I became Willie's universe. He became the parent/father I never had, and me, his fountain of youth. I made him feel young again, and he made me feel grown up. We were both sick.

Trucking

Willie occasionally worked as an independent trucker. He had an old, 15-speed, 18-wheel Mac truck. He delivered soybeans, paint, and other things around the United States. I went with him. We drank coffee and ate handfuls of speed, little white crosses and black beauties. He let me drive the truck one time, but I just didn't have the coordination required.

The Mac had two gearshifts and at times, in certain situations, you'd have to put your arm through the steering wheel to guide it while shifting with both hands. The rig was an antique death trap and Willie drove it like he wanted to be just a memory.

Foosball Alley-1974

Willie and I moved to Robertsdale, Alabama, near Pensacola, Florida, and opened an entertainment center/arcade named Foosball Alley. We rented an old storefront in a dead section of town and leased the machines and tables. Foosball Alley had pool tables, pinball, air hockey, and of course Foosball tables. The majority of our customers were kids, and the rest were migrant farm-workers; therefore, the money wasn't great, but that didn't matter because the arcade only existed as a front for drug dealing.

Late in the evening, after we closed the arcade, Willie would bring out a small car jack and put it under the edge of one of the pool tables. Then he'd jack that one corner up just a couple of inches, and remove two of the screws that attached the hollow leg to the table. With two of the three screws removed, the leg would easily swing out so he could take out whatever drugs he needed for his contacts, and put in the cash from the night's drug sales. He usually only sold pot and mushrooms, but occasionally he also sold cocaine and speed.

Eventually the good people of Robertsdale started forbidding their children to go to Foosball Alley. There were several bad scenes where parents came and removed their teenagers while calling us all sorts of choice names. Robertsdale, a small, poor, and religiously pious town started getting way too hot for us to stick around. So we accepted that it was time to move on. We went back to the Opelika area, where Willie always had customers.

Tell-A-Tale Motel

For a while we were content to deal drugs and party until Willie, who could never stay still for long, had the crazy idea to drive his hard-tail Harley Davidson motorcycle to California. We packed the saddlebags and a backpack and headed west. The Harley, aptly named hard-tailed, was a rough-riding bike, not designed for cross-country travel.

Sunburned and exhausted we limped into Arkansas. Willie was pissing blood while I seethed, barely containing my rage. We pulled into a roadside rest area to pee and hit loose gravel. The bike went down, I managed to kick myself clear, but Willie was all but pinned under the fuel tank. I struggled to lift the bike as Willie pushed, and he finally managed to shimmy out from under it.

That was the final straw for me; I needed rest. I dreaded crawling back on that noisy piece of metal even long enough to get to a motel, but I did. A few miles past the rest stop, we found a hole-in-the-wall place named Tell-A-Tale Motel. The Tell-A-Tale certainly gave *us* a tale to tell. We checked in, unloaded our gear from the bike, and went into our small, dingy room.

I took a long shower. Afterward, I came out of the bathroom and sat on the foot of the bed. We were having a beer and talking about giving up the trip before it killed us when we both noticed the itching. The room was infested with crabs, and we were covered with them.

We packed up and demanded our money back at the desk. I was grateful when the hotel manager didn't argue with us because Willie was already fit to be tied, and I knew he had his gun in his boot.

Although we were exhausted, we went on to the first town with a drugstore and purchased crab-rid medicine. Equipped with our bottle of bug-be-gone, we set out to find another motel. From directions we were given by a clerk at the pharmacy, we found one nearby considerably less seedy than the Tell-A-Tale. After we checked into the new place, and thoroughly searched our room for wild life, we both showered with the medicated wash and changed into clean clothes.

Unfortunately, we could not yet rest. Weary to the bone, we bagged up the clothes we were wearing at Tell-a-Tale and took off again. We found a Laundromat close by where we washed everything that might have been infested with Arkansas' finest. Finally, completely spent, we went back to the room and fell into bed.

This experience ended any necessity for conversation regarding canceling our trip. The Tell-A-Tale was the final deal breaker for both of us; we weren't having fun. The next morning we rented a place to store the motorcycle and took a bus back to Alabama to get Willie's pickup truck. The truck had his name written on the driver's side door and my name on the other. Seems to me that good-o-boys always like to put their name on everything they possess: belts, trucks, and women. We allowed ourselves one day to rest a bit, and then headed back to Arkansas.

The following morning with the Harley tied securely in the back of the truck; we once again set out for California reaching our destination without further incident. Two days later we stopped to visit my daddy and his family in Half Moon Bay, which was not a good idea. After all, I showed up with an old, white-haired guru hippie, older than my daddy and obviously a stoner. I have no idea what we were thinking when we went there in the first place. Thinking wasn't one of my long suits in those days. Following was my norm.

After just a couple of days we went on back to Alabama. While Willie was totally unimpressed, I still loved California, as I had since my first visit at fourteen, but I had realized on that trip that I no longer found Willie impressive.

Logging

Once back in Alabama, Willie decided to go into the logging business with a couple of ole' boys he knew. They bought an old truck with a hand operated log and pulpwood loader and contracted to cut and remove trees from people's property. Willie would not allow me out of his sight because he was insecure and insanely jealous. So he gave me no choice, I had to go to the woods with him every day, and then to the railroad yard to off-load the logs or pulpwood onto railroad cars for shipping.

The truck was really a pulpwood truck, and not designed for logs. When we cut logs, Willie would load them parallel across the carry bed like we did the pulpwood. We had to extend the logs out further on the passenger side of the truck. We did this to avoid knocking on-coming cars off the road, but to counter the imbalance so the truck wouldn't tip over from the weight, we hung weights off the bed on the driver's side. Fortunately, we traveled on dirt or paved back roads to the railroad yard.

We always had an exciting and terrifying journey. If we encountered an oncoming vehicle and had no room on our right, one of us had to stop and wait, or back up. Willie did the driving, and he knocked down a lot of roadside signs and mailboxes along the way.

Every morning I got up first and made breakfast. After we ate, I did the dishes and packed our lunches and water. Those were long days. In the woods the heat would be suffocating, so we tried to get in and out before noon, which means we had to be on the road by five in the morning. It'd still be dark when we arrived at the cut-site, but we'd get started anyway, because if we were still in the woods past noon, it was not uncommon for one of us to pass out from the heat, an especially frightening experience if the person blacked out while using a chain saw.

I worked the loader. One of the guys would pull the tongs attached to the cable that ran from the boon on the rig to the piece of pulpwood where it lay on the ground, and manually connect the tongs to it. I'd slowly work the levers at the rear of the truck bed to first pull the cable taut, and therefore close and tighten the grip on the tongs. Then I'd pull the piece out of the woods and lift it slowly into the air. At this point one of the men would physically guide the piece of pulpwood into position over the truck bed, and once in place, I'd lower it to rest.

Sometimes I'd pull the tongs and attach them to the pulpwood. That was one of the hardest things I have ever done. I had to pull the cable and tongs through dense woods over rocks, roots, and limbs from fallen trees, I found it very challenging physically and hated every minute in the woods with Willie, and as the days passed, I started hating Willie as well. The whole scenario reeked of insanity. By the end of each day I'd often be in tears.

Once we got home, Willie would be done for the day, but my day would not be over for another hour or two. I still had to make dinner and then do the dishes before Willie would allow me to rest. Unhappy and slowly realizing that I was a slave, I wanted out.

I voiced my discontent for a long time, but I was afraid to leave Willie. I knew how crazy he could be. Sometimes when mad at me, he'd throw me to the floor and put his foot on my hair, and then he would sit down and calmly drink his beer, his boot still on my hair on the floor. He would not let me up until I was still and quiet. Once I tried to fight him and he kicked me in the side of my head, my ear rang for days. Because he cut logs he wore steel toe boots, so I'm lucky he didn't kill me. After I calmed down and he let me up, he'd point out how he had to treat me that way because I'd been bad and unreasonable. In order to survive, I'd agree with him and go get him another beer.

After a while, regardless of my fear and a desire to stay alive, it became impossible to be agreeable with such a disagreeable bastard. Even a doormat has her limits. I finally told him, "I'm leaving Willie; I can't live like this."

He responded as I had feared he would. Gun in hand, he told me that I would never leave him, it would not happen, that he'd never let me go. Willie held me at gunpoint for three days. Most of the time, he kept me naked and in bed. He used speed day and night and never slept. As an old truck driver, he was accustomed to little or no sleep for long periods of time. Fortunately for me, the speed also made it impossible for him to have sex. He threatened to kill both of us several times during those three days.

I honestly didn't believe I'd get out of there alive. When I went to the bathroom, he'd insist on going with me. If anyone knocked at our door, he made me stay quiet until they went away. If anyone phoned, Willie would assure the caller that we were just down with a bad cold.

At some point I accepted that it was all or nothing. I couldn't over- power him, so I had to out-con him. I started to *act.* I had a great teacher in my momma, the natural actress. I begged Willie to forgive me. I said I loved him and would never leave. I convinced him throughout the final day of my captivity that I'd realized I could not live without him. I kissed him and begged for his forgiveness. Eventually he bought it because he wanted it to be true.

That's when I went for it. I said, "Come on honey, go to the bathroom with me, I have to pee," and as I had hoped, he said,

"No, you go on alone baby, I trust you."

As soon as the door to the bathroom closed, I climbed out the window with only a towel to cover my nakedness. I went quickly before he even had time to consider the possibility. I did not need to stop and think. I had already made up my mind. All, or nothing.

The closest neighbor lived less than a minute away running, and when I reached their porch, I knocked boldly on the door, having no time to waste and nothing left to lose, but my life. A lady answered, and although I didn't really know her, I appealed to her as a woman. I asked if she could loan me a blanket and let me call a friend for a ride. I offered no further explanation, and she asked for none. While waiting for my girlfriend, I heard Willie's car squealing out of our driveway, and I knew he'd be out looking for me.

When my friend arrived, I ran to her car and we sped away. I felt certain that Willie would be waiting around every corner and would shoot both of us, but we didn't see him. My girlfriend Rae took me to my momma's house. Momma was living in the mill village again and caring for my grandmother, who had breast cancer.

Momma shocked me when she gave me an inexpensive wedding ring that her fifth husband, my brother David's father, had given her. More than anything, I must admit that I was flabbergasted that my Momma had held on to a pawn-able item and that she had not sold it years ago for a bottle.

Momma knew Willie's temper well, so she understood immediately the danger I faced if I did not get the hell out of Alabama. So she gave me the ring and told me to pawn it for gas money. Knowing he'd no doubt come for me soon, my friend Rae and I left immediately. Once again, heading for California.

Mississippi-1975

Rae drove a rusted out old car and neither of us felt too sure about its ability to make the trip. Nonetheless, as fools will do when out of more desirable options, we headed West, making a quick stop at a pawnshop in Mississippi where we were thrilled to get $25.00 for Momma's wedding ring. Fortunately, gas was cheap then, and we had a foam ice chest filled with lunchmeat, bread and other munchies.

Route-66, here we come. I'd be twenty-one in a few weeks and Rae was nineteen. A very quiet, edgy, overweight mousy girl. Her family was as backwoods-backward as you could get and still walk upright. I liked Rae, but she wasn't always easy to be around. Of course the road trip was fun though, two country girls off to see the world. We listened to cassettes, smoked too many cigarettes, ate junk food, drank beer, and smoked pot.

I didn't have a driver's license. I had driven a car a few times and a big rig once, but no one had been willing to take the time to teach me how to drive. Willie wouldn't teach me because that would have given me too much freedom. Therefore, Rae did all the driving, and I read the map, it's amazing that we made it out of Alabama. I had called my sister Deborah from momma's house before we left. She lived in the small beach side town of Montara in the San Francisco bay area and agreed to allow Rae and I to crash at her place for a while. We knocked on Deborah's door on a clear morning the end of June 1975.

I soon had a job, but weeks passed and when Rae could not seem to find work she chose to go back to Alabama. She had not managed to fit in at all and seemed perpetually on the edge. I could not understand though, why anyone would willingly leave California for Alabama.

Willie

I'd been in California for ten weeks, my sister Anne lived with her mom and my daddy in Half Moon Bay, about a mile up the road from where I had rented a room. One morning Anne and I were in a pumpkin field in Half Moon Bay with a girl I had recently met, Tatiana. Tati was taking pictures of the pumpkins and Anne and I had tagged along just for fun. Then to my absolute horror, Willie showed up!

He must have been watching my daddy's house, he knew where Daddy lived from our trip to California the year before, and had apparently staked the place out hoping I'd show up there. Apparently he followed my sister Anne when she came to meet me.

He strolled up to us like he had been invited and insisted that I go somewhere with him to talk in private, I refused. That enraged him. I could tell by his dilated eyes that he had not slept in days. He most likely drove straight through from Alabama to Half Moon Bay.

He assured me that he'd hurt me and I believed him, but I was tired of being afraid and running. I told him to go ahead and do it, that I would not go anywhere with him. I struggled to sound brave, but I was terrified that he'd kill me right there in the middle of the pumpkin field.

Anne and Tati backed me up. They flanked me on both sides and tried to talk sense to Willie. They told him that if he killed me, he still wouldn't have me, and he'd die alone in prison. We stood together arms linked and he finally stormed off in a rage, and we got the hell out of there.

The next day I saw his white Ford pickup truck with our names printed on the doors in a local shopping center. I hid in the bathroom at the Safeway store for a half-hour. Cell phones weren't available then, and I didn't dare go outside to the payphone, so I holed up in the toilet until I could no longer stand the suspense. When I ventured cautiously back out into the day, his truck was gone. I watched over my shoulder and freaked out every time I saw a white pickup truck for over a year. Gratefully, he never came back. Gradually, I began to feel safe.

Chapter Fourteen - Toxic Twenties

T & T

I remained in Montara for two years, where I rented a room and worked at a deli. I met a good man, Gary, a carpenter, and for a while my life seemed somewhat normal. But after almost two years together, Gary decided he needed a major life change. He sold his home, bought a RV, and set off to see the United States. I had by no means seen all the states, but having traveled back and forth across our country many times in my twenty-three short years, I had no desire to hit the road again. So we wished each other well and went our separate ways. When I moved to California I had hoped to find peace, but unfortunately my roller coaster ride did not end in Montara.

After Gary, I moved into Dominic's Hotel in Half Moon Bay. At the time Dominic's was an old dilapidated place, but it has since been beautifully remodeled. In 1977 it's rooms were cheap and all I could afford on the job I had recently taken at a local janitorial service. I worked days and partied nights. My friend Tati, from the pumpkin field two years earlier, now lived in the hotel too, which had a bar and poolroom downstairs. Tati and I would play pool or shuffleboard and because we were Toni and Tati, we were called

T&T, like dynamite. As usual, I tended to be money scarce and full of fear, but overall, Dominic's and Tati were a good time in my life.

Occasionally I ran into this handsome cowboy, Len, at a bar across the street, and the attraction began to grow. Len worked as a printer in San Francisco, but he lived and worked on a horse ranch in Half Moon Bay, where he taught horseback riding. So I had a job, a room, a girlfriend and a boyfriend. I felt more secure than I had ever been in Alabama, but I knew I had to do something more. I couldn't live at a hotel for the rest of my life, shooting pool with Tati, flirting with Len, and working for a janitorial service. My lifestyle was still *temporary* and I wanted permanent.

My sister, Anne, had been teaching me how to drive, and I'd been studying to take my G.E.D. exam. I set out to get my license and diploma in an attempt to better myself and improve my life options, but the possibility of real success still seemed beyond my limited grasp. Thanks to the gentle old man in Albany, New York, who introduced me to the joy and power of reading, my comprehension skills were very good, considering I had been a "D" student who quit school early in the ninth grade.

On November 15, 1977, I took the GED exams and to my astonishment, passed. Barely, but I passed. I did well on reading and comprehension of the Social Studies and Natural Sciences material, and I scored above average in my interpretation of the literary material; however, I tested below average in math. I have always had difficulty with math.

Two weeks after the GED exams, I passed my driving test. For the first time in my life, I felt actively involved in becoming visible. I felt proud of myself but I couldn't afford college. Being only qualified to work as a cashier, cleaning lady, logger, drug dealer or waitress, I knew I had to do more if I expected to ever have financial security.

After a lifetime of false starts and dead ends, I made a huge life changing decision. I decided that I'd join the Air Force. Fed by the recruiters' propaganda, that I'd get an education, have free room and board for a couple of years, and save tons of money, I enlisted. Then I hoped that Daddy would be proud of me, that just maybe for once he'd like me, even if he could never love me. Then I'd be "somebody." I'd be visible. It all made sense at the time.

Uncle Sam- January 19, 1978

The sweet-talking recruiter said I did well on the test. He suggested, based on my test results, that I enter the Air Force and pursue a career as an Aerospace Ground Equipment Mechanic specializing in hydraulics. I didn't really know what that meant, but it sounded great, so I signed up. I told everyone, especially Daddy, "I'm going to be a Aerospace Ground Equipment Mechanic specializing in hydraulics." High on optimism and sure that I'd excel in the Air Force and never have to depend on anyone for anything ever again, off I went onward and upward, to victory.

I signed up, signed in, and scheduled to report for boot camp in eleven weeks. That same day I moved out of the hotel and in with Len, my cowboy. I didn't want to leave Len and soon after I signed up with the Air Force, I began having huge doubts about joining. The day I left for Lackland Air Force Base in San Antonio, Texas, Len drove me to the airport. The cold, gray morning reflected my mood. The realization that I had made an awful mistake engulfed me like the damp morning fog devouring the day. I felt like a cornered animal, but I had no choice, I had signed, I had swallowed the soap.

Boot Camp

I did not tell the recruiter or the Air Force doctors that I had asthma. My health wasn't great, it never had been. I decided to just do my best and try to keep up. The first week of boot camp was hell. I found the whole system to be as insane as my childhood. They set out to tear me down, and it wasn't very hard to do. I went there broken. I did okay for almost two weeks, at least I held my own. Determined to keep my mouth shut and follow the leader, I kept my head down and plowed ahead.

The first thing I saw as we drove through the main gate onto the airbase was a sign that said, "Lead, Follow, or get the hell out of the way." Not being a leader, and since I couldn't turn on my heel and leave, I accepted that I had to follow. The physical exercise proved to be very difficult and I found a lot of the rhetoric hard to swallow. I told myself to hold on, that I had worked harder as a logger.

When they asked for a volunteer I raised my hand because I saw straight away that the girls who tried to hide got singled out for the worst detail. I had long hair. I thought I'd be able to keep it under my hat with the help of hairpins, but I repeatedly got in trouble because a strand of it would escape confinement. One evening I had a gal in my barracks take a razor, we had no scissors, and cut it all off. It looked awful, but I refused to give those bastards something to yell at me about. I was grateful for my drab green hat.

In an attempt to avoid a harder detail I volunteered to direct people to their seats in the mess hall. My job required that I stand, very erect, with one arm behind my back and the other across my abdomen, bent at the elbow and pointing in the direction of the area the Airmen to be seated, were required to go to. Yes, I was a human arrow. Put that on your resume if you want to make a point.

Sometimes I felt like the white trash equivalent of Mr. Magoo, a cartoon character. It seemed disaster and crazy just followed me around, waiting to sabotage me at every turn. So it seemed about right that shortly after I began training at Lackland, they quarantine the base due to an outbreak in the states of the Russian flu. I thought nothing of it since I was stuck on base anyway. I went on about my daily duties as best I could and listened to the girls crying in their bunks at night, dreading the morning. I slept on the lower bed and each morning, in preparation for inspection, I'd crawl under it and pull the sheets taut. That's the last thing I remembered when I awoke in the hospital.

According to a fellow Airman, whom I spoke to days later, I had passed out under my bed. When the T.I. came in to inspect our barracks and found me on the floor, he screamed at me, and when I did not respond, he pulled me out from under the bunk by my feet to find me out cold and running a very high fever. I don't think I had the Russian flu. I do know I had a serious cold, mono, and an ear infection.

The real problem started when I did not get better and my asthma got worse. The doctors asked me repeatedly if I had ever had asthma. I kept answering no and we continued this dance for about three weeks. I felt stronger, but my asthma would not relent, so I finally gave up. I didn't think I could do it anyway. I could not imagine starting boot camp all over again. It's one thing to sign up while in denial, but I had seen how nuts it was in reality and I didn't want to be there.

Defeated, once again a dismal failure, I admitted that I had asthma, and they began the discharge proceedings. They discharged me from the hospital and put me in a unit called Casual, for those of us waiting for discharge or for some matter to be settled. I had daily duties, but also a lot of freedom. I met a T.I. that took me to the clubs at night off base. I always seemed to find the men and the party. I hate to admit it, but in so many ways I am my mother's daughter.

Chapter Fifteen - Men-Moves-Money-Madness

Quest for a Life

Len picked me up at the airport and we returned to Half Moon Bay. In 1979 we moved to Vallejo near his parents. Len still worked in San Francisco and the commute quickly became tiresome for him. I gladly agreed to return to the San Francisco Bay area, Pacifica, in 1981. In 1982 we went our separate ways, in agreement that we just weren't right for each other. Len was a good man, but we weren't a good couple. You need to know when to let go.

Len and I had been over for two months when I met Michael at the liquor store where I worked. I had waited on him several times, and we shared some casual flirting, but nothing serious. One day at the end of my shift, when leaving the store, I ran into him on the sidewalk. He invited me to join him for a drink at the bar next door. We drank and talked, he charmed, he bought, and we were sure it must be love.

I moved in with Mike two weeks later, my life always moved too fast. He worked as a mechanic, but he made most of his money selling cocaine. There were people in and out of our apartment at all hours. It's amazing we weren't arrested. I quit the liquor store, to make time to party. The rest is a big, white powder blur. When Mike wasn't home, I sold cocaine to his clients. I learned how to cut and weigh the drugs, pinching and keeping a bit of each packet for myself. I lost a lot of weight, I didn't notice. People started asking me if I were anorexic.

We led this crazy life for over a year waiting for the shoe to drop, the cops to come, or worse, death. We had a wake-up call when someone broke into our dealer's house while he slept and killed him with a baseball bat, for his drugs and money. Mike worked for a local auto repair chain that had multiple shops in California, so he requested a transfer to another shop sixty miles away. He moved a few weeks later; I did not. This was one of the smartest decisions I ever made in my life.

After Mike moved, I got off the cocaine and my health and weight slowly returned to normal. Normal for me anyway. I took a bar-tending job at a small bar and pool hall for a couple of months. One day I went to work and found a padlock on the door, the owner had been busted. Almost immediately, I found a new job doing the same thing at a slightly larger, older, dive bar down the road two miles, and I just kept rolling. The next several months I moved from one place to another and one man to another. There were moments of happiness and hours of sorrow. There was an instant of hope and otherwise almost constant hopelessness.

I always had more bills than money. In an effort to survive I had three jobs in 1984, bartender, store clerk/cashier, and I worked nights as a switchboard operator at a small answering service. At the answering service I answered phones for a computer supply company, called Pac-Service Center. The owner of PAC-Service, David, often complimented me for the job I did. I was considered the agency's best operator.

One day David called and asked if I'd be interested in working in his office as a secretary. I explained that I had no office experience except on the phone. I did not know how to type, and I had never worked in an office. He said most of the typing would be numbers on an invoice, and he'd teach me. I took the job. It paid more than I had ever made before, $10.00 an hour. I quit all three of my other jobs and felt like I'd soon be a real girl, a visible important contributing member of society.

But financial security would prove to be no cure for the lonely emptiness I carried in the core of my being. I worked, thought I fell in love again and again, I drank and like Momma, I danced as fast as I could, but it wasn't fast enough. The shadows still found me. They blanketed me so completely at times that I could not breathe. Then the day would clear for a short while but the darkness always returned.

Suicide

I'd always considered suicide an option. There were many times that I decided to kill myself, but inevitably I'd choose to hold on a little longer because I knew I could always kill myself later if things didn't get better. I did not fear death, but life scared the crap out of me. Death provided the escape hatch I could choose at any time. I had watched too many people suffer far too long in hopeless situations, only to die alone in sorrow. A coward, I always knew I'd choose suicide in the end if some man or drug didn't do it for me first.

I am not religious. Organized religion scares me more than my government. I often see politicians and preachers as one and the same. They lead with fear and guilt and line their own pockets. War is always in the name of some man's God. At this time in my life I considered myself an Agnostic Spiritualist. I believed there was some truth in all of it, but most of it was crap. This one thing I did consider reasonable, at least for me, that if there were a creator and we were created in the image of the creator, then we are not these bodies, we are not this vulnerable, quivering mass of fear, shame, and guilt that we appear to be.

I wanted to return to a less complicated form in a less complicated place. I just couldn't do this planet anymore. Willing to risk that I might be mistaken about life, death, and God, in the hope that something better might exist or at least, sweet nothingness. I needed to believe that the after place, the place after the body ceases to exist, would be kinder and safer than the place where I'd been for the past thirty-two years, a place where I had never felt safe and had known little peace.

I began going out to the end of the Pacifica pier at night with an old friend of mine, Jose Cuervo. I considered how cold the water would feel and wondered how long it would be uncomfortable, how long would it take until the pain subsided? Every night I'd drink my bottle, but then change my mind, for that day. Then I'd head back to the warmth and false safety of the bar.

July 10, 1986

When I woke, came to, on July 10,1986 I had an epiphany. I awoke aware of the fact that my life would not get better until I grew up, and that I could not grow up if I stifled my emotions and dealt with every situation by taking a drink. I stopped drinking alcohol that day and stayed sober for almost ten years. And my epiphany proved to be correct, without the booze, I had to deal with life and make decisions, and in doing so I grew up. In 1986, when I chose to get sober, I was thirty-two years old but emotionally twelve.

The next three years roared past like a freight train. I left Pac-Service center and took a job as assistant office manager at a counseling agency. Working with a large pool of therapists and psychologists helped me escalate my much-needed emotional growth spurt. One year later I applied for and was hired to work as a secretary at a residential recovery facility. The facility called "The Project" offered a drug and alcohol recovery program for men. The main facility, an old convalescent hospital was located in a park in San Mateo. Like the counseling agency, The Project job contributed a lot to my newly budding self-worth and esteem. I worked there for two years.

Momma Finds Peace

In March of 1989 my brother in Alabama, David, called to tell me Momma had died. Although my heart ached for her life so sorrowfully spent, I honestly felt happy that she had escaped the hell her life had been and hoped she'd finally found the peace that she so desperately sought. For a moment I felt shame that I did not feel sorry that I had lost my mother, but I knew– I had never had her, none of us had.

I thought, now Momma can go to another place, take another form, or even enter sweet nothingness. Anything would be better than the life she had just barely survived for sixty-two years. Go on to peaceful stillness Momma. No more running Sweet Genell, no more fear, no more shame.

Momma's Last Performance

My plane landed in Atlanta and David and his wife Bonnie met me at the gate. You could still meet people at the gate back then, and we caught up on hugs and small talk while we waited for our sister Deborah's plane to arrive an hour later. Deborah lived in Santa Clara and had flown out of the San Jose airport shortly after my flight had left San Francisco.

We caught up with one another on the two-hour drive back to Opelika. Momma's funeral would be the following day. Her brother Gene, a Baptist preacher, had made the funeral arrangements and would lead the memorial service.

Mid-morning, we drove to Frederick's Funeral Home in Opelika, where Momma's body waited patiently, finally at rest. When we arrived, we, my siblings and I, found it odd that so many people were there. Momma had no real friends and her two brothers and their families rarely visited her, but the room overflowed with mourners. Complete strangers, mostly women, were coming up to Deborah, David, and me and telling us how sorry they were for our loss, and how they knew what pain we were in. They encouraged us, no, actually they pushed us, to cry and grieve. They said, "Let it go, go ahead and cry, we know you're in pain, y'all go on and let it out."

Strangers hugged us to their unfamiliar bosoms while forcefully pulling our heads to their shoulders in the hope that they'd be the one we'd fall apart and weep on. When we questioned who they were, they were all members of my uncle's church, and none of them even knew Momma. When I told them that I did not feel sad, they acted as if I had introduced myself as Satan.

Deborah, David, and I wanted a few minutes alone with *our* momma for closure, but the open casket sat on a raised area in the front of the chapel. There were rows of pews with complete strangers seated in them, and more were milling about, attempting to be as close as possible to the grieving children. Like fiendish bodachs from this side of hell, ghoulishly and without embarrassment, feeding on the suffering of others. They didn't want

174

to miss anything. It was like an episode of Jerry Springer. Finally, fed up with being part of the show, we insisted that the funeral director close the curtain that was drawn to each side of the coffin.

As the curtain slowly and dramatically closed, there was a disgruntled murmur that passed through the crowd. They wanted action and public displays of anguish. I admit, I felt pissed off, we didn't know these people, and they didn't know our momma. David, Deborah, and I gathered in the tiny nest of privacy the curtain provided and quietly said what we each needed to say to Momma and to each other. Careful to keep our voices low so as not to be entertainment for the strangers on the other side of the curtain.

I told Momma I loved her but had never liked her. I expressed my anger and told her how much I had needed her. I told her that through my own therapy I could now understand that she was never bad, just sick, and I had tremendous sympathy for her. As a woman I forgave her and I did love her, but the part of me that will always be a little girl still felt such tremendous anger, and I let that little girl tell her so. I wished her a safe journey and peace. I felt good, I felt like the weight of the world had been lifted off the tiny shoulders of my inner child.

My siblings and I rejoined the strangers and were seated for the service, which we did not care for. The service was all preaching and had little to do with Momma. I thought it would never end; my uncle can be long winded when he has a captive audience. Once we

175

escaped from the pretend-to-be friends and mourners, we returned to my brother's house.

As is the norm after a funeral, people came and went all afternoon. Most folks brought food, which we all appreciated because we were emotionally and physically drained.

Deborah and I returned to California the next day and David and Bonnie began a new life, without Momma.

Chapter Sixteen - The Dam Breaks

Marriage - 1992

In 1991, I met Bruce, a tall attractive electrician who seemed to adore me. We had only dated for three months when he proposed and I accepted. I could not believe that I'd finally be the bride! I'd been the maid of honor and a bridesmaid more than once, but never, "The Bride." Not counting my little trip down the aisle at fifteen and by trip I mean acid-trip.

We set the date for August 22, 1992. I felt like a princess. We rented the amphitheater in the redwoods at Memorial Park with log benches for seating and a rough wood platform for the ceremony. Memorial Park has an abundance of large, beautiful redwood trees. It was perfect. I bought a simple, inexpensive white cotton dress and a white circlet of small, silk flowers for my hair. Determined to keep it simple, my maid of honor and bridesmaids wore simple sundresses in cheerful colors. The guys all wore nice shirts and shorts. My brother-in-law and his blue grass band played the music. Friends took photos, and the food/reception was a potluck spread to which everyone contributed.

From the day Bruce proposed to me until our wedding day seven months later, I busied myself with wedding plans and my house-cleaning job. Bruce and I moved into a small studio apartment, and reality began to rise to the surface, but I refused to see it. I wanted my day, my wedding. I had the dress, the place, the hopes and dreams. I allowed myself to believe that what I felt was just pre-wedding jitters, that all would be well as soon as we were married. With happy-ever-after just around the corner, I could not give up. All those whispered wishes on so many shooting stars. It was my turn.

Sadly, however, it turned out that Bruce could not be the prince that I desperately tried to believe he'd be. He was petty and selfish and had a serious problem with rage. It started slowly, one small outburst here and there. He carried grudges forever, and would go into a rage even if he saw one of his ex-girlfriends or ex-bosses driving down the street. According to him, everyone he had ever had any sort of relationship with had screwed him over. He held himself up as a victim.

He never hit me, but he'd destroy things. He'd rip off his shirt or kick the garbage can across the room. He frequently threw his glasses or the answering machine while having one of his temper tantrums, and would then pout for hours or storm out the door.

Occasionally, Bruce's fifteen-year-old son would stay with us for a day or two. One day he made Bruce angry about something, and Bruce threw his key ring with about twenty keys on it at him. It missed his son's head, barely, and hit Bruce's newly painted white van. It looked like someone had shot the van with buckshot. It would have killed his son if it had hit him in his head.

I knew then that I could never live with a person capable of endangering the ones he was supposed to protect, which shows that I was still a pretty sick puppy because I went ahead and married him.

The Wedding

From the beginning Bruce acted detached and disagreeable about all the wedding plans. When I'd call him on it and ask if he wanted to cancel the wedding, he'd insist that everything was fine and that he really wanted to marry me. The day of the wedding, he whined about the shirt, the weather, and everything I said or did seemed to piss him off. But instead of running for the hills, as I should have, I put on my pretty dress and went to the hair salon where a stylist did my hair and adorned it with my halo of tiny white and pale blue flowers.

The redwoods were breathtaking and our friends and family had a great time at the wedding, but Bruce and I were robotic. We just went through the motions. Then on to the beloved honeymoon, which turned out to be a little slice of hell. We didn't go far, we drove up the coast to Santa Cruz. Since Bruce wasn't about to pay for more than one night at a *reasonable* hotel, we spent most of our honeymoon sleeping in his van. It did have a large, raised, comfortable bed, but if you forgot where you were and sat up too fast, you'd hit your head on the roof of the vehicle.

Throughout the night as the exterior of the van cooled and our breathing warmed the inside–condensation would build up on the metal ceiling and begin to drip in our faces, a rude way to wake up. The absence of a toilet in the middle of the night was worse than the lack of headroom and the water torture though. The restaurants we ate at were good, and the beaches were beautiful, but Bruce continued to act like a complete ass. He shut down the moment we said, "I do," and didn't even pretend anymore to be happy.

Over lunch at a beautiful beach side restaurant the day after our wedding, he read the newspaper at the table and wouldn't talk in more than three-word sentences. We were married ten very long sad months that helped to contribute to my mental collapse.

Breakthrough

I had been on an energy quest for years; I constantly struggled with serious fatigue. After I married Bruce, my emotional and physical health deteriorated to the point that I could not get out of bed, sometimes for days at a time. I'd been on a special diet for five years at this time and did not eat beef or pork. I talked to a doctor that I cleaned for and she offered to examine me. She advised me to eat beef; she said that I needed more protein in my diet, and she diagnosed me with Chronic Fatigue Syndrome and Fibromyalgia.

On her advice, I started a high protein diet and a regime of vitamins and nutrients, but my condition grew increasingly worse. Although I had not had a drink in over six years I found myself once again sick and suicidal. I had come full circle. Like a cat chasing her tail, I felt like I had made no real progress, that the past six years were just a really bad joke. Completely spent, exhausted, emotionally and physically. I wanted to stop, cease, die.

I'd been seeing a therapist for over a year at this time, and she knew that I'd been very depressed; she tried to help me, but I kept spiraling downward. I now understood that no matter how far I crawled out from under the white trash heap that I was born into, it would always consume me, define me. There would be no escape.

On a foggy depressing morning I drove out of Half Moon Bay to go to a doctor in San Mateo. I took Highway 92, which is a winding, dangerous stretch of road at any time, but I found it especially difficult to navigate that day because of the endless tears streaming down my cheeks. Weary, I felt like my neck could not support the weight of my head. I considered driving off the cliff, but I was afraid I wouldn't die right away but just lie there instead, helplessly suffering while bugs crawled into my screaming mouth, and the seagulls and vultures pecked out my tear-filled eyes. I wanted to stop the suffering, not create more.

I realized I could not make the drive to San Mateo and I turned around and went home. I called my therapist Clarice but all I could do was tell her over and over again how tired I felt. I knew I had kept the balls in the air for as long as I could, and now they were falling. Clarice suggested that I allow her to call an ambulance for me and that I should stay in the psychiatric unit at the county hospital for a couple of days and rest where I'd have some support. I knew I had to do something and that I could not drive myself, so I agreed and Clarice called an ambulance to take me to the hospital.

As soon as the paramedics left me at the hospital I became agitated and afraid. A nurse had me change into a flimsy hospital gown and then insisted I lie down in a bed in the emergency room. The beds were in an open room, and anyone walking down the main hall could see me lying there. The nurse would not allow me to close the curtain around the bed. I felt exposed and vulnerable.

As is most often the case in a county hospital, the place was a mad house, overrun with a constant stream of patients seeking help. Police with prisoners needing assistance, hospital staff and paramedics and homeless folk just seeking refuge. All of these people were walking by, naturally curious; most were checking out the sick people in the beds. I felt like they had put me in a fish bowl. I became more agitated by the minute. I begged the nurse to ask a therapist to come talk to me, but no one came.

I laid there for over an hour. Finally, cold, alone, and sadder than ever, I got up, located the bag with my clothes in it that the nurse had put under the bed. I closed the curtain so I could get dressed intending to get the hell out of there. I had my clothes back on and while bent to lace my shoes, the nurse came in and told me to get back into the bed. "No. I don't want to stay. I changed my mind. Thanks, but no thanks. I'm going home."

The nurse called in a rude, condescending doctor. He said that since my therapist had called the ambulance for me (although I had agreed that she do so) that they considered me on a 5150, which meant they could hold me for seventy-two hours against my will for evaluation. When I insisted he at least let me talk to a therapist, he said they had to run tests first to make sure I hadn't taken any drugs that might kill me. I pointed out that I'd been there over an hour. If I had taken any drugs that would kill me, I probably would have been dead already.

That's when the doctor called security. With two large security men standing by, the doctor insisted that I change back into the gown and get back in bed. I requested that they all step out and close the curtain while I changed. The doctor refused; he said I had to change in front of the security guards because I had caused so much trouble. I went nuts. I insisted they leave me alone. He told the guards to undress me, and I started to scream "rape" at the top of my lungs.

A female nurse came in and told them to leave and she'd get me changed. Once I'd changed back into the cold, flimsy gown, the security men locked me in a bare, windowless room where they usually kept inmates from jail or dangerously psychotic people. At this point I felt like a limp rag. I wept alone, locked in the hole. I can't remember if I were tied to the bed or just too weak to rise from it.

Finally, a woman from the psychiatric department came in, took one look at me and said, "What the hell have they done to you?"

My rescuer found a wheel chair and took me to the psychiatric ward where several members of the staff tried to comfort me. I told them what had happened in the emergency room and they were mortified. They said they'd been trying to get the medical staff to understand what it's like for someone to come in under emotional stress and be made to strip and wait and go through tests.

One nurse said they were working on having the policy changed so a psychiatric patient could get mental health care first or at least at the same time as the medical intake care. By law, since I was admitted as a 5150, they were required to keep me in the hospital at least overnight for my own safety. But the staff agreed that the welcome I had received had made me so fearful of the hospital that I would not feel safe enough to rest. They allowed me to call a girlfriend to pick me up and drive me home. I went straight to bed exhausted and slept for two days with only the dreams, the awful dreams.

Clean and sober six years, a new bride, and still swallowing the soap.

The Psych Ward

Two weeks later I entered a psychiatric unit in San Francisco. After my experience at county hospital I felt especially terrified checking into another facility. But my condition had grown worse, the dreams were unbearable and followed me into the day, and I'd been completely bedridden for two weeks. I felt weak as a newborn kitten and I had no support at home. That odd survivalist inside me knew that I had to get help, even if it scared the hell out of me to do so. Fortunately, it turned out that I had made a good decision. The hospital in San Francisco proved to be very professional and I had a great doctor.

My doctor said that I was in the middle of a total breakdown. I'd later see this as my *Breakthrough,* but that would take some time and a lot of work. The doctor also reaffirmed my previous diagnosis of Chronic Fatigue Syndrome and Fibromyalgia. Before I checked out of the hospital two weeks later he'd add Post-Traumatic Stress Disorder to the list.

I had one dream repeatedly for the first several days in San Francisco. I found this dream to be the most disturbing of all the nightmares my mind had conjured throughout the years. I dreamed that I was hanging in midair by a rope tied in a noose around my neck. In the dream I felt like a leaf or a feather at the end of a piece of spider web.

Weightless, I'd sway and twirl in even the slightest hint of a breeze. I liked it there and I'd be sad when I'd awaken and find myself once again a captive of an exhausted useless body, a tortured soul, and a depressed hopeless mind. I kept trying to go back to that place of sweet peace.

Under heavy medication, I stayed in bed all of the time; the doctor would even sit by my bed to talk to me instead of requiring me to come to his office. Then as he slowly decreased the dosage, I began to venture forth occasionally to walk to the end of the hall and back to my room. I walked with my head down and would slide my right shoulder against the wall. I felt my way along in this manner, and only knew there were other people present by the sound of their voices and I'd see their shoes as they passed.

Even when someone spoke right next to me, his or her voice seemed far away, in another place. I didn't want to go back to that place; I didn't want to look up and see their faces. I only wanted to go to the end of the hall and then back to my safe bed and my dream. I wasn't going back to their place ever again.

Healing brings strength for dealing; a week of drug-induced rest and I did begin to return, even if unwillingly. After two weeks in San Francisco, I returned to the Coast propped up by Prozac and set forth to see what I could make of the scattered remnants of my life. My therapist Clarice would play a big role in my recovery. Through the work we did in therapy I came to understand how little credit I gave myself, and how I had always labeled myself as less than. Labels like white trash, useless, retarded, a bother, and many other negatives.

Clarice started correcting me every time I used a negative to define myself and suggested I reword things. For example, when I'd say, "I'm stupid," Clarice would have me change that statement to, "Regardless of education, I am intelligent and able to learn."

As I started to value myself, a little bit at a time, I stopped calling myself a drunk, an addict, a rape victim, an over-eater, an adult child of an alcoholic, a codependent, etc. I changed the way I labeled and described myself in an attempt to change the way I saw and felt about myself.

Chapter Seventeen - Geographic Therapy

Sedona

I worked occasionally as a cashier at a friend's gift and bookshop in San Mateo. The shop sold travel videos about special places, and they had one for Sedona, Arizona. I had heard amazing things about Sedona, so I took the film home and watched it. Rich with Native American history the video piqued my interest. The area, with its red rock formations, looked like another world. I felt sure I was meant to be there. So I put most of my belongings in storage, packed up my little Honda civic until it was about to burst, and set off to find Nirvana.

My first day on the road I drove as far as Barstow, California, which is a little over 100 miles from the California/Nevada border. I made it to Sedona the next day. Through the classifieds in the local paper, I found a cheap room for rent and gave my new landlord all but $140 of my money. I had to find a job.

The following day I applied for several cashier jobs at the seemingly endless number of gift shops in Sedona. The huge tourist trade area meant there would be a lot of work possibilities. I found a small job the first day at a T-shirt shop eleven hours a week. It was a start. Pleased with my progress and thrilled at the possibilities in Sedona, I felt scared but very optimistic.

One week in Sedona and doing well, but lonely. You can pack up and reinvent all you want, and yet some things will always follow you, like you, your memories, and for me always the loneliness. I met and talked to a lot of people, but as had always been the case, I felt like no one really heard or saw me. It's hard to become visible when you've been invisible for so long. Lonely and tired of casual, polite conversation with strangers, and eating all of my meals alone, I treated myself to dinner at a popular local restaurant.

I sat alone at a corner table reading the local freebie newspaper that advertises local events, restaurants, etc. and could not believe it when I saw that the photo on the cover was Ray SunStar. I eagerly read the extensive article inside about him and his art gallery in Sedona. I had met SunStar at his art gallery in Sonora, California, two years before. An incredible artist, he is Osage Indian, known as the Tall Ones. I loved SunStar's work from the first moment I walked into his gallery and I had bought one of his prints.

Now, sitting in a restaurant in Sedona, Arizona, two years later, I discovered that Ray SunStar was in Sedona too. It's a small amazing world. The next day I went to his gallery, which is located in an upscale shopping center in Sedona. The building, the grounds, and Ray's art were perfect together. Daring to think I might actually have a chance, I asked SunStar if he needed any help and he hired me to sell at his gallery. For the next eleven months I worked my different sales jobs, met new people, and enjoyed the beautiful area that surrounded me. But I still could not shake the loneliness.

Half Moon Bay - 1994

I gave notice at my jobs, packed the Honda and once again headed west. I missed California. Back on the coast, I moved into a house in El Granada that belonged to my step-mom Lynda. My cousin Jake already lived in the old house two blocks from the ocean and within walking distance of the harbor, and he agreed to rent me a spare room. I had an arrangement with Lynda that my rent would be modest in exchange for my doing the caretaker duties on the property.

A friend told me about a job opportunity in nearby Pacifica working for a one-man company that purchased, refurbished and resold ATM machines. The owner, Len Plant, had been operating the business alone since starting the company five years prior. He had no file system, other than boxes of this and that scattered about the offices. He had grown the business to a point that he needed help. I called, interviewed and he gave me the job. I jumped right in and set up several file cabinets, dividing the files into clients, distributors, personal, and so on. The organization of the files took several weeks. I worked four half-days to begin with, but Len assured me that I'd be given full-time soon.

Len had issues, as did I. He struggled with depression and although attractive and successful, he was terribly insecure. We had a lot in common. Ten years older than I, he drank too much, cheated on his wife, and overworked in order to avoid issues and to isolate himself. I sympathized; I understood. We were frequently alone in the offices, and quickly became friends and confidants. We'd talk for hours about everything and nothing. Len insisted that he'd soon leave his wife. He said that he'd been unhappy for most of the marriage and he wanted out.

I knew Len's wife, not well and we weren't close, but before I went to work for Len, his wife Ruth and I frequently chatted at the mini-mall where she owned a small shop. Ruth had told me many times that she was unhappy in her marriage, however, at eleven years older than her husband she feared starting over again. I never seriously thought she'd let him go, as her fear of being alone outweighed the unhappiness in the marriage.

After a few months, Len admitted that he felt attracted to me. He'd been showing it in many little ways, but it still shocked me when he just laid it on the table one morning. I found him attractive, considered him a friend and I cared about him, but I had no desire to get in the middle of the mess he and Ruth were in. We had a few brief encounters in the office: a prolonged hug, a kiss or two, but we both agreed not to go any further until, and if, he ended his marriage.

Bear - 1995

My sister Doreen had lived in Minnesota for the past several years. She had a dog that she'd had long before she left California; his name was Bear, a gentle giant. I had always coveted my sister's dog. I loved him. A shepherd, husky, and possible wolf mix, a kind and intelligent truly wonderful four-legged gentleman. Doreen phoned me the end of February 1995 to tell me that at the grand old age of thirteen, Bear had gotten a young yellow lab, that she had recently adopted, pregnant. He'd been, shall we say, loving on the pretty girl ever since she moved in a few months before, but Doreen had not believed Bear could get the young lab pregnant, not at his age. Surprise!

Because of my love for Bear, Doreen suggested I adopt one of the puppies. I had not allowed myself to have a pet since my dog Canna died, ran over by a logging truck. I saw myself as unworthy of a two-legged or a four-legged baby. The thought of the responsibility frightened me. Hell, I could barely feed myself at times, but after some thought, the idea of a wiggly, happy, silly puppy as a companion and best friend won out. I had a good job with Len and a safe home in El Granada, so why not?

Blowing Wind

When I lived in Sedona I dated a Native American man Raven Sun. He played a red cedar flute and I found the sound soothing, so before I left Arizona I bought a handmade one for myself. I had never played an instrument before, but I loved the flute. Playing felt like meditation to me. Three months after I returned to California, I saw an advertisement in a local paper regarding an upcoming concert in Davis featuring my favorite flute player, a world-renowned musician. I didn't have to think twice; I went. I had a great seat near the front. His music was wonderful, I left a bigger fan than before and I signed up to be added to his mailing list.

Soon afterward I received a flier about a flute class being offered and taught by this man at a one-week retreat in Montana in June of 1995. I did not consider attending because of the cost and the fact that it'd be in Montana. But after talking to Doreen, I found myself toying with an incredible idea.

Bear's puppies were due the end of April or the first of May, and I intended to drive to Minnesota to pick up my new buddy since I'd never allow my puppy to travel in the cargo hold of a jet. I didn't want her first experience away from her birth family to be terrifying. One morning it occurred to me that I could drive through Montana, attend the class, and then drive across Canada and drop down into Minnesota. I rationalized that I had a good job with Len, and I'd soon be full-time and on top for sure.

Montana - June 1995

I discussed my plans with Len and he agreed to let me take time off to go pick up my puppy. We arranged for a temporary worker from an employment agency to work in my absence. Len also gave me extra hours the next few months so I could pay for the flute class, gas and on-the-road expenses. As the day to leave drew closer, I became more excited, and I realized that it was a good thing that Len and I were taking some time away from one another; we each needed to sort out our feelings.

On the long drive to Montana, I toyed with the idea of a future with Len. My mind fumbled clumsily with the thought, coming at it from different directions, but I couldn't convince myself that it would happen. I could not convince myself that it *should* happen. So I did the one thing I had always done well, I kept moving, driving a mini-van I had bought a year before. I needed the van because of chronic fatigue. It served as a rolling bed. Whenever I just couldn't keep going, I'd crawl into the back and take a nap.

One day before the flute class started I arrived in Montana and spent the night at a KOA campground. Whenever I stayed in a state park or a campground, I made it a habit to tell nearby campers my situation, that I was traveling alone. I preferred older people in RV's. I'd ask them to keep an eye out for me. Not only did I find that people were more than willing to help, they usually brought me over food or firewood and often invited me to join them for a meal in their campsite as well.

People like to feel needed, and I always let them know I appreciated it. This little bit of human contact made the loneliness on the road bearable for me. I love to take long road trips, and I suppose I got a lot of my need to roam from Momma and her rambling attitude, but I have never been comfortable with the loneliness, the alone-ness.

The next day I checked in at The Feathered Pipe Ranch, where the class was being held. The rustic resort was used mostly as a yoga retreat and fully staffed by their regular crew of cooks, maids, groundskeepers, etc. I shared a room with three other women. I liked all of my roommates, and everyone at the retreat was upbeat and open. But I immediately realized that I should not have been there.

All of the other students were musicians and several were music teachers. I had called the coordinator of the class months before and he had assured me that I'd do well, that I needed no previous music experience to take the class offered. But by the end of the first day, after listening to numerous fellow students play their flutes, it was obvious that they were better already than I ever hoped to be. Nonetheless, I had paid a lot of money and traveled a long way so I decided to make the best of it.

After the first two classes I initially decided I would not participate in a recital scheduled for the sixth day of the workshop. I clearly did not know how to play, and being surrounded by a class full of great musicians, I saw no reason to humiliate myself.

However, as the day approached, the others lovingly encouraged me to take "my" moment. As they pointed out, I paid for it. I'd been practicing a brief piece I'd made up one morning while sitting in the early morning sun. I'd go off by myself to practice, embarrassed by my inability to play. Since I don't know one note from the other, the piece I wrote was not an actual tune but a mournful little ditty that I had played over and over again in order to remember.

People from nearby Helena were invited to come to the retreat to hear the students perform the pieces they had composed. A makeshift recording studio was set up in a cabin, and each student given a few minutes' recording time, a memento included in the price of the workshop. The day before the recital I decided that I would do it, I'd just do my best and not take to heart what the strangers from town thought of me. So I took my turn in the recording cabin and when I had finished my piece, the man operating the equipment said, "that's it?"

For the recital I donned my prettiest outfit, a long, purple dress with fringe and beads. I painted my fingernails and sat with my class. I would not play for the locals. I would play for myself and those people who had encouraged me. When my turn came, I introduced myself and explained that I did not know anything about music and that I offered just a simple tune, but it was mine and I would share it. I received a warm and sincere round of applause after I performed, and I felt glad that I had taken "my" moment. The next day I said goodbye to my new friends and left for Minnesota, puppy bound. I had no idea at the time how much that slobbering fur face would come to mean to me.

Gheen, Minnesota

Gheen, Minnesota, in my opinion, is about as close to absolutely nowhere that you can get. My nephew had to catch the school bus before the sun came up to make it to school on time. In the winter, the below-zero freezing temperatures were unbearable; in the summer the multitude of bugs, thanks to the thousand-plus lakes, were even worse than the cold. I arrived at Doreen's house on June 26th where I immediately fell in love with a four-legged fur-face that would come to be known as The Goose.

The almost-white little girl had a gentle intelligence that she clearly inherited from her daddy, my old friend Bear. Bear looked like a shepherd/husky/wolf mix and the mother was a yellow lab. We had expected lab-looking husky shepherd babies, but Mother Nature had other plans. There were nine puppies, and five looked just like the mother while four looked just like Bear. I wanted a male that looked like Bear, but my sister convinced me that the males that looked like him did not have his attitude or intelligence. She had told me, over the phone, about the little white/yellow female that was her father's daughter.

At Bear's advanced age, he was impatient and easily annoyed by the wild and silly puppies. He kept them in line and at a distance with his booming bark and frequent nips. However, he allowed this one little white fur ball to sleep cuddled safely between his huge paws. The other puppies were too aggressive for the gentle one, so her daddy protected her. The moment Doreen pointed The Goose out; I knew she was the one for me. The other puppies were wonderful, playful, happy little bundles of joy, but The Goose was a breathing picture of love, gentleness, intelligence and peace. I loved her from the first time I held her near my heart, which she proceeded to steal and heal. Immediately I knew the universe had brought a great teacher into my life. We never know when the teacher will come, or in what form.

I'd been sure that my teacher would be the famous Native American flute player in Montana, but I'd been mistaken. My greatest teacher turned out to be a tiny white being whose poop I'd gladly clean-up for the next nine years, and in that nine years she'd teach me how to love and how to allow myself to be loved.

The Goose

The Goose – April 23, 1995 / February 16, 2004

The Goose and I got to know one another over the next ten days as we slowly drove back across the United States, staying at state parks and K.O.A. campgrounds. I took my time on the return journey, enjoying my new companion. I didn't want our alone time to end. Although anxious to introduce The Goose to Len and friends, I almost regretted having to share her because no one had ever adored me like she did. I didn't want her to fall in love with someone else and therefore love me less. That would be the first and the greatest lesson The Goose ever taught me. When love is genuine and unconditional, it is unlimited. I quickly learned not only to share The Goose with others but I delighted in doing so. The more love she received, the more she gave, and the more I learned about how love works.

We pulled into California a couple of days before my birthday in July. I was not due back to work for several days, so I spent the first two days home unpacking the van and getting The Goose settled. I called Len at the office several times to let him know that I had returned and to see when I could stop by to show him The Goose. I found it strange when I repeatedly reached the office answering machine. The temporary secretary should have been in the office.

With each message I left, I became more concerned. Early morning, my third day home, I went to the office and was surprised to find the secretary there. As it turned out, she'd been allowing all of the calls to go to the answering machine, as she had been instructed to do by Len, after he had a heart attack and was hospitalized. She told me that Len would be going into surgery in about half an hour, and the odds that he'd make it were slim.

I rushed to the hospital and arrived while Len was in surgery. I sat there with his wife and comforted her when we were told Len had died. I didn't get to see him again, he never met The Goose, and I didn't get to say good-bye. This was an awkward, awful time.

Len's wife turned to me, as she knew very little about his business or associates. I helped her conclude his affairs and clean out the offices. Len's wife and I were both surprised to find a telephone Len had locked inside his bottom desk drawer, a phone that neither she nor I had ever seen a bill for. After some digging we found the bill and uncovered Len's secret love affair. It was soon obvious that Len had a lot going on.

So I no longer had to make a decision about Len, whether we should stop where we were or go forward, or if I wanted to be involved with him at all other than professionally, but I also was out of a job! Len had assured me that I'd be working full-time before the end of the year. He also had promised me full health insurance coverage, a must with my ongoing physical and emotional problems. Although childish, I felt abandoned again. Len did not leave me, he died, but it still felt like another abandonment, another dead-end.

Chapter Eighteen - Internet Love

Web TV

A local help wanted ad caught my eye, caring for an elderly man on the coast. I drove to Half Moon Bay to meet Raymond and he hired me on the spot. Landing a new job right away helped soothe my newly abandoned heart. I enjoyed Raymond's company and the job proved to be very rewarding. When not at Raymond's, The Goose kept me company and filled my days and nights with laughter and play. I hung out at the Happy Cooker Restaurant in Half Moon Bay, where I'd socialize, write, and read at my usual table that served as my desk away from home. I cannot say that I was not happy. I often felt happy, but the loneliness that had plagued my life still clung to me like a heavy wet tee-shirt.

Some days were truly intolerable and my nights painfully long. I kept up a good face for the outside world, but I couldn't fool myself. With each passing day I became more grateful for The Goose. That silly fur-face was my heart, but she couldn't fill all the gaping holes in my life, but she tried to.

I took a second part time temporary caregiver job. A Hospice care nurse that I knew asked me to help out as the patient, Rose, had little time left but her illness had been long. As will often be the case, her family had been with her around the clock and were exhausted and needed respite. I have always been comfortable with death; after all I considered suicide my back-up plan. I accept death as simply being a natural part of life. It does not frighten me. It's life I don't get. It's life that frightens me.

I took the job and gladly spent time with Rose during her last few weeks in her broken body. It turned out that my lack of religion enabled me to comfort and empower those in the process of passing. I can allow people their beliefs, regardless of what they may be. I kept Rose laughing. I hope someone is there to keep me laughing when it's time to pass.

Rose took her leave with such grace and dignity that I felt a great gift had been given to me, in that I had a moment of her precious time. Her family had treated me with such love and gratitude and when I packed up my things to say farewell, they surprised me when they gave me a Web TV unit that had belonged to Rose. They said she had instructed them to give it to me after she departed. Little special thoughtful moments can save a burdened heart from a million breaks.

I didn't have a computer so I really appreciated Rose's kind gift. I took the unit home, hooked it up, and in no time at all I found myself in the huge amazing world of the Internet. Next I did what comes naturally for today's single gal; I went straight to online dating.

Cyber Outer-Space

What a strange place Cyber-space. I delved into a whole New World. Being online for the first time at age forty-six is an eye-opening experience. Once comfortable with the process, I couldn't get enough. I found job opportunities, political opinions, sites set up just for bitchin', restaurant coupons, and, of course, the personal singles sites in abundance.

I love Craigslist. Craig introduced me to another realm. Once I found the Internet, I felt like there had been a parallel universe within arms-reach that I had been completely unaware of. I couldn't get enough. I posted my first personal ad on Craig's list. Later I explored a couple of those pay-to-play sites. But I found the free postings I put on Craig's list always generated more response and positive outcome than all of the cost-you-money-for-your-honey sites combined.

There were times when I'd receive numerous responses daily, but I only met a small fraction of those guys. For one thing, the longer I communicated with a man by email or phone, the more he'd turn me off. I grew tired of obsessive questions about my body, my sexual desires, and my breast size. I think a lot of guys out there never intend to actually meet any woman; they just want a little phone/computer sex while the wife is watching Wheel of Fortune in the next room.

Even worse and a really big yuck, which always led to my flamboyant use of the sacred delete button, was when the man would describe his penis. It seems these guys all took the same class in "Send her running 101" because most of them used the same phrase, well-endowed, when describing themselves. This is way more information than a lady needs before she's even had a cup of coffee with you.

Delete.

My ads clearly stated the following:

No married men, even if you are thinking about leaving her.

No men younger than me, I want a man at least close to my own age.

No hardcore religionist, of any faith.

No political fanatics, of any party.

No bigots or cigarette smokers.

And please don't contact me if you are looking for a Barbie doll or arm candy.

I choose to be a man's partner, not a possession or an ornament.

If you are about what you have, what you drive, what you do, or whom you know, please do not write to me.

Even with it all laid out in black and white; the following is what I most frequently received in return:

I'm married, but I'm willing to give up my wife for the right woman.
I am a Christian, but I'm willing to give up Jesus, for the right woman.
I am a smoker, but I'm willing to quit, for the right woman.

And if these charming proposals didn't hit pay dirt, they'd tell me about their Corvette or Harley, how big their bank account was, or that they personally know this celebrity or that one. Oh yeah, and let's not forget the constant stream of twenty-something guys that wanted me to teach them how to be a man. They all insisted they were very mature for their age, and "well endowed."

DELETE, DELETE, and DELETE!

I did get together with several men, one at a time of course. We'd meet at a coffee shop or a bar, and sometimes–although not a good idea at a restaurant. I quickly learned that the first time you meet a new person, plan to have a cup of coffee or a glass of wine only, no movies, long walks, or meals on the first date. Do not think of the first meeting as a date at all. The first meeting is only to determine if there's chemistry or at least a comfortable level of communication and common ground between the two of you. Then, if there were some of the aforementioned, and only then, arrange to go on a date.

Although still awfully lonely, I must say, having all the emails, phone calls, first encounters, and occasional dates at least kept me busy and gave me less time to feel sorry for myself. Overall, I found the whole process enjoyable, entertaining, and very educational.

The Fisherman - 2003

Sometimes you don't need the Internet, things happen the old fashion way, you actually meet someone in the flesh. On a cold January evening I walked into my home away from home, the Happy Cooker Restaurant in Half Moon Bay. A couple of regulars I knew well asked me to join them and I did, glad for the company. As usual, the conversation quickly deteriorated into a good-hearted and raucous political discussion. We all agreed on the basics politically, but we'd nonetheless rib one another just for the sake of argument.

When Martin walked in the door, a burst of laughter met him. The source of the outburst our table. I had never seen him before, and I would have remembered because I found him very attractive. He paused at our table and remarked in jest that we were out of control, and asked what was so funny. We told him what we had been discussing and laughing about, and as it turned out, he could be quite the devil's advocate. Months later I'd sometimes get angry with him as he had the ability to provoke me into heated discussions about all sorts of things, but I actually enjoyed his playful prodding. We had many enjoyable debates.

That night at the restaurant we asked Martin to join us, and the rest of the dinner became one of those few really great times you have in your life if you're lucky. The kind of occasion you want to write about on a special piece of paper and hide it in a secret place. We all sat together long after the meal had been consumed, talking and laughing. No one seemed eager to see the evening end. Eventually my friends said good night, but Martin and I remained another half an hour, lingering over our wineglasses. When the waitress started clearing tables in an effort to close for the night, Martin walked me out to my van where The Goose sat waiting, tail wagging, and we continued our conversation, standing in an almost empty parking lot.

The night had turned bitterly cold, especially in contrast to the cozy restaurant. We soon gave in to the chill and said goodnight, but not before Martin gave me his card and told me where his boat was docked in the harbor near my house. I had trouble sleeping that night. I lived so close to the harbor that berthed his boat that in the still of the night, once the noise from the traffic on Highway One had quieted, I could hear the low, mournful sound of the foghorn repeating its warning call to ships entering the breakwater. That night, every time I heard the foghorn, I thought of Martin on his fishing boat docked in the harbor, and I wondered if he might be thinking of me.

Martin told me a lot about himself the first night we met. He came to Half Moon Bay every year to fish the crab season and would move on afterward to fish the salmon in Canada. He had a daughter in California that he tried to see as often as possible, although things were often uncomfortable with him and her mother.

We had very compatible social and religious beliefs, but our political lines differed greatly. Of course, being on opposite sides politically did give us hours of interesting, although often heated, conversation.

The next day The Goose and I walked out the pier and easily located Martin's boat. I watched him selling crabs to the throngs of eager consumers who go to the harbor during crab season to enjoy the bounty of the catch. The crabs were in wooden crates submerged in the water beside his boat. I wasn't sure what I'd do or say if I did find him, and once I did, I found myself frozen with indecision. Martin was good with the people. He had them all talking and laughing as he had had us doing at the table the night before.

I stood apart from the crowd an observer not a participant, as often the case would be, and watched him jump from the front of the boat to the deck. He pulled one of the crab-laden crates up out of the water by its tether rope and started loading several of the wiggling, pinching crustaceans into a white bucket. As he stood to dump the crabs from bucket to bag, he saw me standing there behind the crowd and warmed my heart when his face betrayed his happiness at seeing me. The fear that had me frozen motionless in that spot disappeared immediately, replaced by the same comfort and ease I'd felt with him the night before.

That night we drove down the coast to Pescadero where we shared a wonderful seafood and pasta dish, homemade bread, and dry wine. The conversation, the same as the previous night, flowed effortlessly and I found it invigorating. I had to admit that I was hooked on the fisherman. Martin didn't actually lie to me but he didn't tell me the whole truth. His clever half-truths left me to believe what I chose to believe from the information he gave. In hindsight – in other words after we slept together – I had to admit that I had never asked him if he were still married. Even after I realized that he was, at least sort-of, I tried to convince myself otherwise.

Martin never referred to her as his wife, but as his daughter's mother. He had been careful to avoid conversations about home and talked more about living and working on his boat. I suppose because otherwise I must be very stupid and I am not, that I knew or at least suspected all along, but I wanted him. I wanted to laugh and play and make love. I'd been lonely too long. I settled. It's easier to use the delete button online. It's hard in the real world when he is standing right in front of you in flesh and blood.

I wish I could say I stopped seeing him as soon as I found out the truth, but I didn't, not right away. I would intend to say "no" the next time he called, but I'd say "yes." "Yes, make me laugh, make me feel, just one more time help me to pretend that you won't be going away soon." But I knew he'd be going away. Crab season would end in June, and so would we. I couldn't face going back to answering ads and writing emails, making phone calls, and meeting one man after the other, always busy with the process and never simply enjoying a man's company and attention, and even if I had wanted to go back online, I couldn't.

Two months after Martin and I met, my computer (I had replaced the Web TV unit with a real computer) had a nervous breakdown and everything on it was reduced to non-sensible gibberish. I'd been actively working on *Alabama Blue*, which I originally titled *Southern Discomfort*, for over a year. I had 107 pages written. I had slowly become more comfortable with the computer and the direction my book was going. I had dreamed of writing my memoir for twenty years. So when my computer crashed I felt devastated and foolishly I had not backed up my work on disc. Like a young lover that is certain her love would never hurt her, I really never considered that *my* computer would crash. It's one of those things that you just don't get until it happens to you.

I lost it all. The only sections I had left were pages I had started with over a year before when I had childishly thought that I'd write my book the way the great authors before me had, with pen to paper. A friend gallantly tried to repair my computer and restore my book, but he could not. Therefore, my two main distractions from a lonely life were no longer available to me. My Fisherman, and my beloved Internet. That's a lot of loss when you have little to lose.

At least I still had my sweet Goose and a job. I'd been taking care of Raymond for almost three years, but I still barely made ends meet financially. I had nothing set aside for the future and I saw no way possible for me to save money, much less buy a home of my own. I was getting older by the day; sometimes it just felt like I couldn't catch a break.

One night, alone, missing Martin, I phoned my brother David in Alabama. He still lived near the mill village we grew up in but out in the county in an area called Beauregard. He had four acres and on the property was two trailer homes. Both of the homes were pretty old and in need of repair, but David had been slowly working on them since he bought the property.

By the time I called David that night, broken-hearted about Martin, my lost book, and my lack of a future, I felt like I was out of options. I guess I needed someone to suggest a direction that I might go in, but when David suggested I move to Alabama, well, I didn't see that coming!

Return to Rotten Roots

David made a good case. For starters, he pointed out that my nieces were almost grown, and that I had rarely seen them, much less been a part of their lives. In addition, two years earlier he and Bonnie had given birth to a baby boy, my nephew Sully, who coincidentally was born on my birthday July 18. Since I felt so lonely and fearful about my future, David had me thinking with his proposal.

His next selling point was the straw that broke the California girl's back. David gave me the second trailer that sits on his property. It needed cleaning, painting, and some general repairs. It had not been lived in for several years. They used it for storage. However, it had two bedrooms, a full kitchen, living room and bath, and he promised to help me fix it up. He was right that I should move to Alabama and I knew it. Most months I could barely pay my bills, and I knew that I'd never be able to buy a home in California.

David knows that I'm not crazy about Alabama, so he understood moving there would be a hard decision for me to make. I really wanted to be near my brother and his family, my family. I really, really wanted the security of my own home and the freedom to do with it as I saw fit, no more renting and sharing and trying to be invisible. From there I talked myself into it. I saw nothing but positive.

I said to myself, so what if I don't fit into that community? I will just create my own community. I thought, there must be some open-minded, fun people in Alabama. I'll find them on Craig's List! The Goose can run free. We will live in the woods near a creek. I will have the spare bedroom for an office and a studio. I will have more time and less pressure, so I can finally focus on writing and art. Maybe the best place to write Alabama Blue was in the South where it all had begun.

I convinced myself that although my brother's property is a good drive from town, that I could always go into nearby Auburn. Surely there would be jazz clubs, good restaurants, plays, and other activities that would interest me there. After all, Auburn is a university town. I might have been born a mill village girl but in the thirty years I had lived in California I had come to enjoy, to require, diversity, art and an open-minded culture.

The more I considered it, the more it made sense. It's unbelievable to me now that I actually convinced myself that it would be okay. Especially in light of the fact that I had revisited Alabama several times in the past thirty years and had never once enjoyed being there. I loved seeing my family, but the weather, bugs, mosquitos and cigarette smoke everywhere you went, bigotry, fear, ignorance, and religious fanaticism made me crazy! When in the South I had to watch what I said and to whom. I was always getting into heated disputes with people about my views and theirs regarding almost everything.

The last time I had visited Alabama, I'd been told more than once that I'd most definitely be going to Hell because I had a pro-choice bumper sticker on my car. I had another that read, "I believe in separation of Church and Hate." That one made me very popular. There were a thousand reasons, and I knew what they were from my own experience, that Toni Pacini should not move to Alabama. But I did anyway.

I wanted to believe that I could make it work. I thought it'd be easier to let go of Martin if he were 2,700 miles away. I loved my job but the man I took care of was a big guy, and he had very little ability to stand or do much of anything else on his own. I knew I couldn't keep doing the heavy lifting required to transfer him from bed to chair, to car, to toilet, to exercise mat and so on. My knees already were damaged, and I'd had surgery on both of my feet in the past three years and I still struggled with fatigue and depression.

If I could no longer work, what would happen to me? I had no one to care for me so I had visions of becoming a bag lady and eating out of garbage cans. I suppose, considering what I feared to be the alternative, Alabama sounded pretty good and after all, the only option on the table.

Saying Goodbye

I gave a five-week notice at my job and started packing. The next three weekends I had huge garage sales and sold over eighty percent of my belongings. I couldn't take it with me or afford to ship it and I needed the money. As I sorted through my treasures making two piles, one to keep and another to sell, I thought how ironic that at last I'd have the extra room I had always wanted for a workshop/office but I couldn't afford to take my belongings with me.

Ray, the man I took care of, and his wife had limited parking in the development where they lived, so eight months earlier when Pam bought a van to make transporting Ray easier, she decided to get rid of their 1988 Suzuki Samurai Jeep. The jeep had sat largely untouched since Ray's stroke years before. I occasionally borrowed it when my van was in the shop, and Pam knew I loved it. It wasn't in the greatest shape, and it was old, but I love a stick shift. When I bought my van, I traded in my Honda Civic 5-speed because I needed an easier drive, and the van gave me a place to rest if need be. My chronic fatigue dictated a lot of my actions at that time.

When I drove the jeep I really enjoyed the synchronistic relationship between woman and engine. I love to shift, don't ask me what that's about. So Pam floored me when she gave me the jeep. I loved it, the insurance was minimal, and if my van broke down I wouldn't be stuck without a vehicle. That's how I happened to have two vehicles to take to Alabama, which was very fortunate because I couldn't afford a U-Haul. Also if I'd had to carry everything in the van, I would not be able to sleep in it. I wanted to be able to sleep at parks if needed since I'd be leaving California with limited funds. I had to be prepared for anything.

So I had a hitch put on the van and hooked the jeep behind it. I'd fill the section behind the back seat of the van and the whole jeep to the gills. For easy access I'd keep my suitcase, maps, purse, and personals in the front passenger seat area of the van. The Goose would own the back seat and half the back floor area; the other half would hold our ice chest.

Departure day, I hit the road nervous about the van's ability to pull the jeep and all the stuff I had packed in it. When I first took off, the pull felt awkward, and braking was downright frightening. On my way, but terrified I would not make it out of town, much less across seven states and 2,700 miles. I drove the five miles from El Granada to Half Moon Bay and stopped on the side of the road on highway 92 in front of the Happy Cooker Restaurant. I walked across the street to the hardware store for a security chain and lock for the tow-bar. I'd been advised to have a chain in place, just in case the two vehicles managed somehow to disconnect from one another. Yikes!

While in the hardware store, I received a call from Martin on my cell. We were still talking from time to time and he knew I planned to leave that morning. His manner on the phone annoyed me. He spoke as if it were any other day. But when he realized I had already hooked up the vehicles and set out on my journey, he seemed surprised and I realized that he had convinced himself that I would not actually go. He insisted that I wait for him.

When Martin arrived fifteen minutes later I not only felt glad to see him, because of my feelings for him, but also because I'd been fighting with the chain I had just bought at the hardware store. I could not get it properly attached to the vehicle and tow-bar. With his assistance we soon had the vehicles secured. Prepared for a tearful farewell, Martin surprised me when he insisted that he'd drive the first few hours behind me to make sure everything was working okay with the vehicles. I quickly and gratefully agreed. Especially since the road I had to take out of Half Moon Bay consisted of several miles of winding, uphill travel. I figured if the van could pull the jeep out of Half Moon Bay, the rest would be possible. It was a welcome relief to know that if the jeep could not make the pull, I had someone behind me.

The van did great and I felt a lot calmer and more optimistic when I got to the top of Highway 92, and onto the 280 freeway. Martin followed me for several hours until we stopped in the small town of Wasco, where he suggested that we check into a motel and call it a day. I did feel exhausted, just getting out of town was emotionally and physically draining, so I accepted Martins offer. And honestly, although he remained one of the main reasons I had decided to leave, I longed for one more night with him.

The evening, understandably bittersweet, passed too fast. The next morning, once I had the van ready to go, Martin handed me a plain white envelope with my name written on it. He insisted I not open it until later. I foolishly allowed myself to be excited. The envelope felt fat, I was sure Martin had finally said all the things I had hoped he'd say over the past several months. Hope springs eternal. Oh, what a silly girl I could be sometimes!

I drove a few miles to a fast food restaurant and parked in the back of the lot. I went in and bought a breakfast sandwich and coffee, took a pee, and then returned to the parking lot where I sat down on the tow bar between my two vehicles and tenderly opened my letter from Martin. The letter that would at least validate how important I was to him and that he'd miss me, and at best, the one that would say he planned to get a divorce and come and rescue me from the dragon's lair.

To my horror I only found one sheet of paper in the fat envelope with five words carelessly scrawled on it: "Take care of yourself, Martin." The rest of the bulk was fifteen $20.00 bills and three $100.00 bills, I felt like a hooker. He had validated how he felt about me, and it hurt. I know he did not mean the money to be for sex; I think he genuinely cared about me, but I wanted so much more. I always looked for love in all the wrong places.

After a good cry and a few minutes wallowing in self-pity, it was time to do what I do so well, shut up, buck up, and keep moving. I emptied The Goose, (let her pee) tossed the breakfast garbage, checked the van-jeep rigging, and set out for parts too well known. I left that parking lot with a new determination to make Alabama work for me because I felt I had nothing to go back to California for.

Tornado Road

Near the end of May 2003, Goddard Space Flight Center reported the following: "During the first ten days of May, more tornadoes occurred in the U.S. than during any other ten-day period previously recorded." There were three hundred tornadoes from the first day of May through the tenth. Fifty people died, and hundreds were injured.

You might say I literally drove into the 'eye of the storm.' Maybe I should have seen it as an omen, but I was too busy dodging the tornado's path to notice the irony. I had increased my cell phone coverage before I left California. I needed the security of knowing I had the phone in case of an emergency. The customer service representative I spoke to when I upgraded my package had assured me that I'd have cellular service all the way across the country because they have towers everywhere. She lied. I rarely had service.

My phone would ring; it rang a lot because people in California and Alabama were seeing the weather reports on the news, and they were concerned about The Goose and me, but every time I'd answer it, the signal would drop, and I'd lose the call. This cost me valuable time and money. I had to repeatedly pull off the road into a rest stop or town, locate a pay phone, call for my messages and return calls. Not a simple matter with a vehicle in tow.

I looked for places with a parking area large enough to park in a way that I could get back out, careful not to pull into the wrong place because I could not back up. If I got stuck, I'd have to disconnect the vehicles from one another, turn them both around, line them back up just right, and then re-hook and re-chain them. I paid a man $10.00 to help me the first time this happened, my second day on the road, and I was determined not to do that again.

I set a goal each day to travel a certain amount of miles and went for it. On the eighth of May I intended to make it to Oklahoma City, but having hit heavy traffic and bad weather I decided to stop sooner. I did not want to drive into a big city during commute time with my rig so I stopped for the night about twenty-five miles outside of Oklahoma City.

I checked into a motel, took The Goose for her unwind walk, and picked up dinner at a little wagon-wheel style restaurant across from the motel. My intention when I crossed the street was to dine in the restaurant, but when I saw all the pickups with gun racks in the parking lot and the colorful group of locals inside, I changed my mind. There seemed to be religious symbols on every square inch of the interior of the restaurant, even in the bathroom. I left with a to-go order fifteen minutes later, glad I had made the decision not to eat there. I felt like I had entered another country.

In the motel room, I opened a cold beer, fed The Goose, and sat down at the little table by the bed to have my dinner. While I ate, I turned on the local news to check the weather forecast for the following day and was grateful I had stopped in the twilight zone after all. On the screen they showed the Motel 6 in Oklahoma City, the one I'd been heading for, flattened by a tornado. I wouldn't have been there early enough to be in the motel when the tornado hit it, but I sure would have driven into a mess.

I stayed at Motel 6 anytime I traveled because the price is usually reasonable and most locations accept pets. I'm afraid that even Tom Bodett couldn't have "left the light on for me" that day. A couple of days later, I limped into Opelika. My brother David met me in town, and I followed him out to the country where he introduced me to my new home. I stayed in David's spare bedroom for the first few days while I cleaned and painted the home I'd spend the rest of my life in.

200 Lee Road

After the Civil War, Opelika's city charter was revoked for abetting the rebellion against the United States–today they would be charged with treason and terrorism. Nonetheless, in 1866 Alabama's citizens voted Opelika the county seat. Technically, this was not possible because the city was unincorporated and without a charter, but they did it anyway. Soon after the war ended, if it ever really did, the Alabama state legislature created a new county out of parts of Macon, Russell, Chambers, and Tallapoosa counties, and named it after the Confederate General, Robert E. Lee.

The Lee name has spread across Alabama like the wild Kudzu plant and Wal-Mart super stores. My home was on Lee Road at number 700+. I won't say what number exactly for my family's privacy, but number 700 indicates that there are over 700 Lee Roads in Lee County. There are schools, churches, and an endless number of businesses named after Robert E. Lee.

The confederate flag still flies at many homes and businesses, especially in the rural areas. I went into several restaurants and service stations and would refuse to spend my money there when I saw the confederate flag inside. I always told the owner, or clerk, why I refused to do business with them. Although I doubt it did any good, it made me feel better.

In an act of defiance during the struggles of the 1960's to end segregation, Governor George Wallace raised the Confederate flag over the Capitol dome in 1963. The controversial flag flew as a symbol of pride for some and a symbol of oppression and hatred for others for the next thirty years. A case filed on December 1, 1992, demanded it be removed. The good people of Alabama won the case on January 4, 1993, and the flag was lowered to the delight of all right-minded humans on the planet.

When I would say anything about the confederate flag, most of the people in the South that I talked to would say, "Lady, that flag's been flying over Alabama's capitol for over a hundred years, and anyone tries to take it down will do so over my dead body." When I'd foolishly point out that it had only been raised for thirty years and that the Alabama Supreme Court had it removed from the state capitol ten years prior; they all simply denied it. Why do people insist on fighting about something they don't even value enough to actually get the facts about?

Alabama

I tried, I really did. Thanks to the multiple yard-sales I had in California I had a little money to play with when I got Lee County. The trailer, or manufactured home (that's what trailer owners insist you call them) that I moved in to, was really dirty. The home had not been occupied in several years, and there were dirt-dobbers, wasp nests, and bugs I never identified, in abundance. I cleaned, scrubbed, and washed every square inch and hauled away load after load to the dump station up the road. We had no garbage service. We hauled it all out, burned, or buried it. My brother helped. He built a ramp to my little front porch because the rains over the years had washed the soil away and left quite a steep drop-off.

I moved in as soon as I felt that I had gotten the place as clean as it could be. Officially moved in, I started the real repairs and painting. It took a while before I got around to unpacking. The little place looked pretty good. David found me a nice used couch and a chair. I bought a bed and a dining room set on credit and hung my pictures. I lined the drawers and shelves with paper, and settled into "home." All of this took six weeks.

Almost broke and completely worn out from the move and renovating my home, I declared it time to relax and enjoy the fruit of my labors. I wanted to connect with people; I tried going to Auburn's *hot spots*, but understandably–since it's a college town all of the people I met were barely in their twenties. That's when I decided to consult my old friend Craig. Even Alabama has Craig's List, so I started looking for jobs, entertainment, people active on issues I support, and of course, *men*.

I met a couple of guys, but our personal interests, political views, and life goals were light years apart. I found no available work; the students in Auburn took a lot of the local jobs, and as will be the case in any economically depressed area, there were very few jobs available for domestic or caregiver positions.

Everyone I did meet seemed to offer the same advice, no matter who I talked to in town or online about a job, fun, or meeting men, they all told me: "Go to church." It became clear that there were only two social hubs in my area, church or bars. I tried to entertain myself at home and spent time with The Goose, but all of my grand plans for enjoying the country were short-lived. First, forget the long walks on the meandering country roads. Everyone had big dogs, and most of them had never been allowed in the house. People kept dogs as guard animals, and they were allowed to run free. Scraps out the back door are cheaper than a fence I guess?

The Goose and I couldn't get a block from our house in any direction without being attacked. This really confused The Goose, as she was accustomed to socialized pets. She could not understand why all those dogs wanted to attack her. We couldn't go for walks in the woods either, because of snakes, chiggers, and abnormally huge horse flies that would land on your face and refused to be swatted away.

The bugs were not the only ones attacking me, eager to take a bite out of my ass. Almost every time I went into town, I'd be confronted by at least one indignant local who'd take offense to my bumper stickers. David suggested I remove them from my van, but I refused to believe that I lived in a country where I had to give up my right to freedom of speech and opinion in order to coexist in peace. One particularly offensive attack came from a woman in the parking lot of a local store. While I loaded grocery bags into my van, she pulled up beside me and literally jumped out of her car screaming,

"Murderer, you're a murd-er-er!"

She introduced herself with great pomp and self-glory as a good Christian. She informed me that she was appalled by my pro-choice bumper sticker and asked how I could promote murdering children. I had heard this speech and several rants like it over and over in a dozen little towns all the way across country and since I'd arrived in Opelika. I usually responded with, "It's a free country; I can believe and support whatever I please," and I'd walk away.

But this time was too much. She really pissed me off. Tired, jobless, covered with chigger and mosquito bites from head to toe, lonely, horny, and completely fed up with bullshit, I let her have it. The martyr drove an old, ratty four-door car with bald tires, and had it filled to overflowing with young children. A small baby in a carrier lay on the front seat, and the other three were sitting or standing in the back seat. None of the children had a seat belt on; they were eating French fries and drinking soda, and momma was smoking a cigarette.

I frequently saw children standing up in moving cars and riding in the back of pick-up trucks in the South. In a lot of the areas the laws to protect children are just ignored and people smoke everywhere; children's lungs are not considered. Obesity is at record highs, and most people are too poor to properly feed their children, but they buy cigarettes instead of birth control. Fed up with the self-righteous repeated judgments placed on me by strangers, I said, "Yes, I believe in choice. Unlike my mother I have a choice whether to carry or terminate and I have exercised that choice. I am not ashamed of my choices. But if I were you, I'd be ashamed of the choices you have clearly made. You apparently chose to have more children than you can take care of, and you drive them around in a car with four bald tires and without seat belts or car seats in complete disregard for their safety. You smoke in front of your children, and I'd bet my life that you smoke inside the home and the car with them present.

You are most likely shortening the life of most of them and creating health problems for at least one of the four. Even worse than the damage you do to their bodies is the darkness you put in their hearts by teaching them to scream at strangers in parking lots if you do not agree with their life choices. And you do all of this in the name of Jesus. You need to learn to live what you preach and take responsibility for your own actions."

Okay, maybe I didn't say those exact words, but pretty close. When I finished my little speech, she replied, "You are going to burn in Hell, and Hell is too good for you!"

Reality Check

David said he wasn't surprised when after only two months in Alabama, I sat him down and told him I couldn't stay. I think the nice lady in the parking lot helped me break down the last wall of my denial. I knew I'd have to sell everything I had left to make it back to California. But to stay would be to sentence myself to hell, and that crazy woman was right about one thing, hell *was not* good enough for me. I had to be in a saner, safer place at any cost. I realized I'd rather live in a cardboard box and eat cat food in California than to have a mansion and filet mignon in Alabama.

I spent the next three weekends at a huge flea market in Dothan, Alabama, just north of the Florida border, and I sold almost everything I had left of my life's possessions, including all of the furnishings I had accumulated for my new trailer. In spite of all the garage sales in California before my move, I had held on to some decent jewelry, CD's, and an assortment of other sale-able items. I'd also shipped at least a dozen boxes of books, mostly new reference books, to my brother before I drove out. These items all sold easily, mostly to the regular vendors at the market.

On the 17th of July, the day before my 49th birthday, I left Opelika, heading north intending to go visit my sister Doreen in Minnesota, before I went back to California. I'd stay with her until the first of the month when I'd receive a small check that would get me the rest of the way. I had promised to visit Doreen after I got settled in Opelika, so I felt like I really should go see her while on her side of the country. The first day on the road I made it to Madison, Alabama where I checked into a Motel 6. The Goose and I parked near our room and walked over to a deli/store next door and bought a sandwich. When we returned to the room, another guest at the motel and his dog were outside, and of course, The Goose had to say hello and cop a sniff.

Before I allowed her to do so, I opened the door to my room, put my sandwich inside, and even walked over to the far bed stand and laid my wallet on it, as I was too smart to leave it on the table by the door. I'd normally put my wallet under the bed pillow or somewhere out of sight. I have been around some pretty underhanded people most of my life and learned the hard way, and after all I am the child of an alcoholic, raised to be hyper-vigilant. But I left my wallet out that day to remind me that I needed to write the day's ATM debits in the register before I put it away.

Feeling secure I went back to the door with The Goose so she could say hello to the dog next door. My room was on the ground floor on the corner of the building. As the dogs socialized, I took a few steps away from the door. There were people all around, it was broad daylight, and I was within six feet of my door at all times. The dogs had their jollies, us humans did our own interaction ritual, and within five minutes, The Goose and I returned to our room. I fed The Goose and then settled in with a soda to enjoy my sandwich. I had only taken one bite when I noticed the empty space on the bed stand where my wallet ought to be. My heart pounding, I told myself, 'Stay calm; you must have moved it. It's definitely here somewhere. Calm down.'

I looked everywhere. I even went out and searched my car although I had just had my wallet at the deli and had not returned to the van since. Then I searched the room a second time. I finally accepted the obvious; I'd been robbed. I called motel security, and the local police arrived within twenty minutes, but the thief was long gone. I had $20.00, cash in the van, but everything else was in my Wells Fargo account and there are no Wells Fargo banks in Alabama. I was devastated. I called the bank and canceled my debit and credit cards, and closed my account. The gal I spoke to at Wells Fargo said they'd have to mail my new account information, and it would take a few days, but I was on the road! All I could do under the circumstances was have the bank send everything to my sister's house in Minnesota.

I told myself that I could make it on $20.00, that I'd just stop at flea markets on the way to Minnesota and sell whatever I had left to pay for gas. I already had a list of all flea markets between Alabama and Minnesota, and from Minnesota to California; they were my back-up plan if anything went wrong. Well, something had certainly gone wrong. On the list I located a flea market near Madison; I had no choice but to go there first thing in the morning.

The next day, my 49th birthday, I drove out of Madison with a heavy heart. On the map the flea market looked fairly close to Madison. I drove for over an hour and feared I had taken the wrong road, so I stopped and asked a man outside of a gas station for directions. He said that I was going the right way. Relieved I started out again. It was six in the morning, the market opened at nine, I had to get there and get set up. I had a couple of boxes of things that had not sold at the Alabama market, but I needed time to pull out some more stuff from the items I had hoped to keep; I had to make some money.

The road became increasingly rough, back road, and I'd been about to give up when I came to a four-way intersection in the middle of nowhere. On three of the four corners, there was absolutely nothing, and I saw more of the same in every direction I turned. On the forth corner sat a large, barren concrete building. It looked like a huge, dirty, windowless box. Behind the building I found a rutted mud hole of a parking lot and one car. I thought, 'Oh crap, don't let this be the place.' Of course it was.

The back door stood open, and I entered with trepidation. I had no idea what I might be walking into. A lot of places in the South have no windows, which helps with the heating cost in the winter and the outrageous cost to run air conditioners in the summer, nonetheless the dim light in the building's interior added to my mounting anxiety. I felt a little better when I saw dozens of permanent sales booths set up, covered with tarps or blankets.

I located the driver of the one car parked in the lot who turned out to be the manager of the flea market, and he agreed to let me set up for the day and pay at the end. The cost for a space with a table was $20.00 for the day. I spent the next two hours gleaning out all of the things from my van and the jeep that I felt I could part with. By nine, quite a few people had shown up and were opening their areas for business. I began to hope that although the location seemed too desolate to attract a crowd that maybe people would come from near and far, maybe I'd make a few bucks. I wish I could say I had been right.

There were very few customers that day, and most of the people seemed to stop just to have something to do; no one was buying. I spent the day talking to other sellers, and most of the people were very compassionate about my experience the night before. The manager came over several times and all but apologized for the lack of business. I made a few sales, but at the end of the day, I had made $40.00. I'd hoped to be able to stay at a motel that night and then head for my sister-in-law's parents' house in Kentucky the next day. They'd let me stay the night, and I could go on to the next flea market in Indiana, but I didn't make enough money. I'd have to sleep in the van at a rest stop and save the cash for gas.

There are some good people on this planet. When I went to pay the manager the $20.00 I owed for rental of the space, he refused to take it. Again, grateful to strangers. With the $20.00 I had started the day with, I now had sixty and some change. I knew, barring any new obstacles, The Goose and I would make it to Kentucky. I loaded up my remaining goods and hit the road at about five-thirty that afternoon, wearing a new necklace made with black onyx beads that the lady in the next booth had given to me as I was leaving.

I cried when she said, "Happy birthday honey; everyone deserves a gift on their birthday."

I sincerely appreciated everyone's kindness but as I drove off up that barren road I felt so damned alone. The Goose and I found a state park that charged $8.00 a night and we went for it. At least there were families camping there, making it safer than a rest stop or an empty parking lot. I awoke before the sun, exhausted, and we headed for Kentucky.

Chapter Nineteen - Limping Home

Kentucky — July 20, 2003

Tennessee is an odd-shaped state. Slender and wide, it's a long drive if you cross it from Arkansas to North Carolina, but fairly easy to cross from Alabama to Kentucky although mountainous at times. I hated burning the extra gas climbing hills pulling so much weight, but I had no choice. We fortunately had no new problems and arrived at my sister-in-law Bonnie's parents' home in the early evening on July 20th. I had met Nora and Bill a couple of times in Alabama when they were visiting. They opened their home, fed me well, and allowed me to rest for a while. I felt so tired, more of a weariness of the soul than the body. The previous four days felt like a lifetime plus two. No actually, the previous four months felt that way.

I detested having to do it, but I called Daddy and Lynda and asked them to send me $200 by Western Union, so I could get up to Doreen's in Minnesota. After my experience at the last flea market I was afraid to even consider moving on from market to market in the hopes of making enough to keep rolling. I assured them that I'd send them a check for the full amount as soon as I got to a Wells Fargo bank.

Wells Fargo had assured me that they were mailing my new ATM and debit card to Doreen's house, and unlike most of the South, there are Wells Fargo banks in Minnesota, so I'd be okay if I could just get there. Daddy and Lynda agreed and I received the money two days later. I admit I was hesitant to leave Nora and Bill's. I felt so alone out on the road, but not wanting to overstay my welcome; I loaded up the morning of Saturday the 26th and hooked the jeep to the van. After hugs and expressions of gratitude sincerely expressed, I took my leave.

With The Goose in her place and all systems go, I started the van. I let it warm up a bit, and then I pulled the gearshift, located on the steering column, down into drive. I felt a small click, and the gearshift went limp in my hand. It had broken and I would not be going anywhere. I laid my head on the steering wheel and cried. The Goose started whining and licking me, trying to be of comfort, but I shattered into a million tiny shards of sorrow.

I sat there for a long time before one of Bill and Nora's sons came out to ask me what was wrong. He convinced me to go back into the house with him, and again Nora and Bill were kind and supportive. Later that morning they had my van towed to a relative's repair shop. The next morning Nora and Bill introduced me to Tony, and he checked out the van. Tony discovered that the rod from the shifter that ran down through the steering column had actually snapped and could not be repaired. He offered to call around to the local junkyards and see if he could find a replacement part for me.

With no other choice, I went home with Nora and Bill to wait, grateful once again for their hospitality.

Tony phoned the next morning and said he had found a junkyard that had a van with the part I needed still attached. Unfortunately, though, he could not go and pull it off the wrecked van for me until the next day. It was Sunday and the junkyard was closed. I asked what the part and his labor would cost, and Tony said the part was $120.00, and that he'd do the labor for $60.00. Back to square one, broke again. On Monday, Tony retrieved the part from the junkyard for my van's repair. Tuesday afternoon, driving my jeep, I followed Nora and Bill back to Tony's shop.

Tony's wife joined us, and we all talked for an hour or so while Tony and his helper finished the job. While we lingered there and without my knowledge, either Nora or Bill told Tony that I'd just asked my daddy for a loan, which he sent to me, and that I only had slightly more money than what he was charging me for the part and repairs.

When it came time to pay, Tony asked me for $120.00 instead of the $180.00 he had asked for originally, meaning he and his employee had done the labor at no charge. For a lonely wandering broken woman, I certainly had my share of good fortune and met some incredibly kind people.

I hooked the van to the jeep, loaded The Goose, and headed north. I had enough money for gas and food, but not enough to go the distance, especially if I had any new problems. So I reluctantly headed for the next flea market. I drove I-65 up through Kentucky, always climbing, pulling my load. I stopped at a small Kentucky market and stayed there for two days and nights, grateful that they allowed the vendors to stay set up and park by their table overnight at no additional charge. This was fortunate for me, but it turned out that I'd be the only one staying overnight. So I did what I always did in rest stops; I made sure to go pee before dark, and unless it was super urgent, I would not leave the van until sun-up. My strategy being that if a nosey person did not know for sure who or what was in the vehicle, man, woman, gun or dog, he'd be less likely to risk messing with me. I sold enough to see me on down (actually up) the road, but just enough.

The Goose and I left Kentucky and crossed into Indiana bright and early on Friday, August 1. We pulled into the next flea market that night and set up for the next day's sale. At every market I found myself pulling out more and more of the *special* items that I had had no intention of selling. The more desperate I became, the less important those treasures and trinkets were to me, and if I were real lucky and sold well, maybe I could even sleep in a motel in a real bed and have a shower instead of sink baths at gas stations.

I did okay at that market. I sold just enough to go on to the next one. I did fairly well at all of the markets, but didn't make enough to really cushion me.

On August 3, I pulled into a large market in Bunker Hill, Indiana. I had sold enough of my larger items, books, baskets, pictures, pots, and pans at the markets, which made it possible to condense my remaining items into a smaller space.

So when I pulled into the Bunker Hill market that morning at sunrise and saw that it was a large market in a well-populated area, I made a big decision. I located the manager and rented a space for the day. After I set my items out on the table provided, I cleaned everything out of the jeep and made two large signs: "JEEP FOR SALE - As Is- $600.00." I cleaned the jeep inside and out as best I could with spray glass cleaner and paper towels, took a deep breath, fed the dog, and hoped for the best. I sold the jeep that day for $500 and the tow-bar, which I no longer needed, for $60. The Goose and I found a clean motel as soon as we left the market, and I took myself out for a huge rare steak.

The next day we drove nonstop through a corner of Illinois and a little slice of Wisconsin, then on into Minnesota. We stayed at a motel in Minneapolis that night and arrived at my Sister Doreen's house early the next morning. Without the jeep the van now felt overwhelmingly crowded, and although The Goose loved her bench seat, I decided that it had to go. Doreen rode shotgun and directed me to the local dump, where I released the locks and slid the seat to the edge. Together Doreen and I tossed the seat out the side door into a large Dumpster.

On the fourth of August, the check I'd expected was deposited to my new account and I acquired a few temporary checks. I immediately mailed Daddy and Lynda a check for the

$200 they had wired to me in Kentucky. I stayed another week to visit Doreen and when I left Minnesota my heart and my van felt a lot lighter. Minus one jeep, a tow bar, my back seat, a wallet, and most of my worldly possessions, I realized that I didn't care, none of that mattered. I was going home.

We made it back to Half Moon Bay on August 27, 2003. The Goose and I went straight to the beach. I had no idea what my future might hold, but I knew this much for sure, I did not, do not and never will, belong in Alabama. Alabama makes me blue.

Happy Cooker

I had dinner at the Happy Cooker and The Goose and I slept in the van that night at the harbor, listening to the sound of the foghorn and awakening to the cries of gulls. Hotels and motels are expensive in Half Moon Bay, and I needed to save the last of my money. I did have a plan, not an absolute dyed-in-wool plan, but an idea of what I'd do next. I'd take a live-in caregiver job although I normally hesitated to do live-in. I had decided that I could handle it for a few months, and it'd give me room, board, and salary until I got back on my feet.

Over coffee at the Happy Cooker the next morning I talked to a friend who worked as waitress there and she offered me a place to stay for a couple of weeks until I found a job. I moved into Kristyn's home on the 29th of August where I stayed for exactly ten days. I took a residential caregiver job in Los Altos. I'd have preferred to stay on the Coast, but I took what I could get. Little did I know at the time, but that job would be one of the hardest I ever had, yet that move would be the best one I had ever made.

Los Altos

I took a job as a live-in caregiver for an elderly man, Lou. He was still fairly mobile but required a wheelchair from bed to couch and to the toilet. The job would require that I be on duty from Friday morning at 8:00 am. until Monday morning at 8:00 am., an eighty-four-hour shift. I could go to my apartment at night, which adjoined the main house, but I had to listen to a baby monitor seven nights a week even on my days off. Since my apartment was attached to the main house, I could go home and check on The Goose frequently.

The apartment was clean, furnished and comfortable. I could eat at the main house when I fed Lou, and the pay was good. I had to take the job. It was just what I needed at the time, although I knew I could not, would not, stay for more than a few months. The schedule was awful, and I did not like to live where I worked.

Stuck there on the property most of the time I could not go explore and socialize, and I did not have friends in the area to come visit me. Having The Goose was, as always, a lifesaver. My best friend, companion, confidant, entertainment center, and a huge hunk of my heart she may be, but she could not fill all the empty spaces, and she could not be everything I needed. So, I went back online.

I started posting ads on Craig's List again, in the personals. Ads on CL are free, but at that time they only stayed online for ten days, so you had to renew them frequently. I'd post an ad, receive a boatload of responses in the first two days (that's always the case) and then I'd play with those for a week or two, sometimes more. As I have said before, most people who respond to ads seem to be just lonely or bored and have no intention of ever meeting anyone. After two or three emails, I'd suggest we talk on the phone, or meet. Some guys would, but some would repeatedly make excuses and keep writing emails. I would not continue these online email relationships. It has been my experience that they never go anywhere.

There would be a few men interesting enough to meet and a few adventurous enough to get excited about meeting, but it rarely worked out well. We might enjoy a cup of coffee, but, usually, I'd be interested and they were not, or they were and I was not. It's tough to find the right combination. I kept posting though, because the emails, phone calls and occasional dates kept me from going insane.

I started working on *Alabama Blue* again, too. I had rewritten the first 100 pages that I had lost when my computer crashed almost a year before, but I found it difficult to focus on my writing. I worked the Los Altos job for five months, and I posted an average of one ad on CL each month during that time. I ran my last ad in January 2004, two weeks before I left the job. I had given a one-month notice and although not certain where I'd go next, I had to get the hell out of there.

I still struggled with depression and fatigue on a daily basis, and that job and my tiny, lonely apartment were swallowing me up, one gulp at a time. I knew that without major change, soon, I'd surely disappear. More financially secure than when I had returned from Alabama six months before, I knew I could at least afford to rent a room while I found a new job. I looked at a few share rentals and found myself considering one in San Jose. I posted work wanted ads on CL and bulletin boards for caregiver, house sitter, pet care, and Jill of all trades. I had a few nibbles, and I felt confident that I would find something.

Then Annie contacted me. She had seen a flier I posted in the El Granada post office on the coast near Half Moon Bay; I still had my post office box there. Annie had a lovely home near the post office and two sweetheart dogs. She needed someone to house and pet sit while she was out of town for two weeks and I could take The Goose along. The Goose and I love the coast so of course I took the job and the money she offered had been generous.

Annie would be leaving in two weeks, and my current job would end a couple of days before she left. The timing was great. That's when Walt entered the scene. That's when life, as I knew it, ended forever.

My Last Singles Ad

I had posted my latest "Looking for Love" ad on Craig's List a week before I met with Annie regarding the two-week job at her house. My ads had grown increasingly creative and more to the point as time passed. I had honed and polished the best way to state what I was looking for in a man. I appreciated the distractions the responses provided, but I had grown tired of the games, lies, and outright bullshit. The title of my last posting reflected my apathy.

"I WOULD NOT DATE A MAN THAT WOULD ANSWER MY AD."

I wanted to see if anyone out there was actually paying attention, and I knew that anyone who got the joke I had borrowed from the Groucho Marx line, "I wouldn't join a club that would have me as a member," would at least be in my age range. Tired of the thirty-somethings looking for an older woman to teach them, or most likely to take care of them, the toxic religionists, and the married smokers; although of course they were all *well-endowed,* delete, delete, I rolled my last dice.

My ad went on to clearly state my case. Several men wrote just to tell me what a bitch I was, but I didn't care. If he wasn't an available, stable, non-smoker who didn't play games, and would not require me to praise him or his God, I was not interested.

Then Walt wrote to me. He sent a photo with his first email, which was uncommon for the first correspondence, and I appreciated his straightforwardness immediately. He appeared to be intelligent, well-educated, financially secure, hard working, well dressed, and straight up. On top of all this, I found him very attractive. I had to get rid of him!

This man could really hurt me. He was clearly too good for me and would figure it out sooner or later, whereupon he'd most certainly break my heart. Surely no man as real and decent as Walt appeared to be could ever want me. For both our sakes, I felt I had to be honest with him, and I felt certain that he would then go away. I reluctantly wrote him back,

"Dear Walt,
Thank you so much for the nice letter; you are obviously
a great guy and I find you very attractive. However, I
have to be honest with you; I am afraid our
backgrounds, education, and lifestyles are too different
for us to find common ground. You are dockers and
loafers, and I am jeans and moccasins. I wish you all the
best.
Be happy,
Toni"

Walt won my heart with his reply. He had me from that moment forward:

"Dear Toni,
Those are just clothes!
Let's not let that stuff determine who we are or whom
we choose to be with.
Warm regards,
Walt"

I sent him my phone number one minute after I read that email, and he called me later the same day. That was January 19, 2004. The next night we met at Molly McGee's on Castro Street in Mountain View. I arrived at the bar early, wearing jeans and mid-calf moccasins. I ordered a glass of wine and chose a seat that afforded me a clear view of both the back and front door. Excitement surged through me like electricity; I felt good about this one, but I'd been wrong before.

On time, he ambled in and I immediately liked his manly, yet somehow boyish gait. He moved his six-foot-plus frame comfortably, and seemed more down to earth than I had expected. He wore jeans, but he still donned the tasseled loafers he'd worn in the photo he had sent to me. I saw him as a man, who could be comfortable in both worlds– work or casual, because he was comfortable with himself. The talk came easily, more so than it ever had with a man before. Walt's eyes are a distracting blue, and I loved his smile. Secure and assertive yes, but not pushy or demanding. I felt safe with him immediately, and trust has never been easy for me to do.

I didn't want the night to end, and apparently, Walt didn't either. He asked me to join him for dinner. We walked up Castro Street, side by side, in animated conversation, and chose an Italian restaurant. The dinner, wine, and the company were all perfect. After dinner we walked slowly back to our cars, not wanting to say goodnight. We walked closer than before and allowed an occasional brush of one's arm or shoulder against the other. It felt electric. It is so amazing when it's right, and it was so damned right. I went back to my little apartment floating on a cloud.

The only bad part was that Walt would be going out of town for several days on a business trip, and that gave me cause for concern. A lot of married men or players use the "travel for work card" to explain why they can only see you once every week or two. Walt hadn't seemed the type, but I still felt wary. My fears were soothed when Walt emailed and called me several times over the next few days. The day he returned we went out to dinner, and the following day we went to a movie. We held hands during the movie; it was totally high school the way we so casually happened to be resting our arms on the shared arm rest, hands almost touching, but not quite. When he took my hand, I felt as if I had finally found home.

During this time of heavy dating, I packed in preparation to put my belongings in storage and to evacuate the Los Altos apartment. I had less than a week before I'd go to the Coast to house sit for Annie. Still uncertain of where I'd go or work after that, I was

246

glad when I received a call from a previous employer and friend of mine. Billi asked if I still worked as a caregiver; I had taken care of her mother-in-law for a few weeks a couple of years before, and I said,

"Yes, I still work as a caregiver; what you got for me?"

Billie had an elderly relative who had recently gone into a Hospice program who needed help. He lived in Pescadero and would be staying in his own home where his granddaughter and other family would care for him, but they couldn't do it alone. I said I could start on Monday, the sixteenth of February, my last day at Annie's. This was great. I'd go straight from Annie's to the Pescadero job. Billi said they would like to have me stay a day or two at a time, to give the family a break. When I told Walt about the hospice support job, which I assumed would go on for several weeks or even months, he suggested that I stay with him in between. Thanks to Billi and Walt, I had just bought myself some more time; surely by the time the Pescadero job concluded I'd have a good place lined up to move to.

On Sunday Walt met me near the storage facility I had rented to store my belongings and we had breakfast. After breakfast I would unload the van into my storage unit and I still had a little cleaning to do at the apartment, but we arranged to have dinner later that evening. It was my idea to have dinner at his place and rent a movie because I knew I'd be exhausted by the time I finished in Los Altos, and I had to be at Annie's the next day. Walt agreed eagerly, which pleased me greatly. When he kissed me goodbye in his car behind the restaurant, I filled up inside like an Easter balloon in a big city parade.

I went back to the apartment to finish up, and although busy I felt giddy with excitement. This would be my first time at his home, and our first time really alone. Oh my, could the night live up to a lonely gal's daydreams? I sure hoped it would. Little did I know how incapable I was of even imagining how happy I could be; I suppose I had nothing to measure it by.

I found Walt's home simple, wonderful and inviting, just like Walt. He welcomed me warmly, and we had a delicious dinner he had prepared of baked chicken and yams. Then we settled in on his couch to watch a movie, I forget which one, and the rest is history, our history, what sweet history. I didn't stay the night, partly because I left The Goose at the apartment, and largely because I was afraid that I'd mess everything up somehow if I did. So I went to Annie's the next morning to stay for two weeks, and Walt left for six days on a business trip in New York. I missed him already.

Being at Annie's felt great, with no one watching my every move, no one to bathe or feed or cater to. I had breathing room and three dogs to play with. I could come and go as I wished; I did not have to get permission or make arrangements. I felt giddy with freedom. Annie's home was breathtaking, built on the side of a steep hill with an incredible view of the ocean and the harbor. I could hear the foghorn at night, and although I knew Martin might be down there, I didn't care. Why would I want a man who was so unavailable, when I had Walt in my life?

Although beautiful the house wasn't very comfortable. There must have been a million stairs. The detached garage set up by the road, and the front door was about fifteen steps below it. A very large living room, dining room, and a fantastic kitchen with all stainless steel appliances were on the first floor, a gourmet's dream kitchen. To get to the master bedroom you had to go down two more flights of eight stairs each, a total of sixteen. Off the sprawling bedroom was a huge bathroom with a sunken Jacuzzi bathtub and an ocean view.

Continuing down what seemed to be a bottomless hill two more flights you would find a lovely spare bedroom with a private bath and a hall bathroom, Annie's office, and the laundry room. Off the office stood a small back porch and you had to go down another twenty or so stairs in order to reach the yard. Now, the doorbell rings. Run! It could be rather infuriating, not to mention exhausting. Annie had a large Rhodesian Ridgeback, Lucy, definitely an Alpha female. The Goose and Annie's male dog, Joe, played well together and sometimes Lucy would join in for a moment, but she snapped at The Goose a lot and kept her on a short leash. This made things a little stressful, but overall, we were all having a good time.

With the exception of the master bedroom, all the floors were hardwood, which looked lovely but offered no traction or cushion for a human's foot or dog's paw. Lucy and Joe were accustomed to the one hundred-plus stairs from the living room to their bathroom area in the back yard, but The Goose was really in pain after a couple of days, as she tried to keep up with their every move. To tell the truth, I felt pretty sore myself but it had been harder for The Goose than it was for me because she ran the stairs, as the other dogs did, and would slip and slide since she had no traction with her toenails on hardwood.

Walt returned from New York on Monday, February 9 and drove straight over to the Coast for the night and returned to Sunnyvale the next morning for work. After work we met at a brewery near Half Moon Bay and then made dinner at Annie's. The next morning after Walt left, I phoned The Goose's veterinarian in Half Moon Bay and told her about the hardwood floors and the pain The Goose was obviously experiencing.

The Goose had been to the doctor two weeks before for a physical, blood work, urine test, and the whole nine yards and the vet had found her to be in excellent health. Always in the past, when she had pain, I'd given her a small dose of children's liquid Tylenol with the dropper. Like the time the horse kicked her in the head. But I felt concerned, she was getting older, and I wanted to do what was best for her.

The doctor said she'd have some medication waiting for me at the counter. Later that morning when I stopped at the clinic, the doctor's assistant said,

"Give The Goose one of these pills each day for five days in her food. If she stops eating, stop them immediately and bring her in."

I said, "Whoa, wait a minute, why would she stop eating; what is this stuff?"

The assistant called the Vet out from the back, and she assured me the medication was perfectly safe, but that it would occasionally upset a dog's stomach. She said,

"If it doesn't agree with her, she'll stop eating, and we will discontinue it and try something else."

I almost said "No thanks," but unfortunately, I did not. I started The Goose on the pills that day, and her appetite seemed unaffected.

Walt stayed home for the next couple of days, tired from his business trip and running back and forth to see me, but as I would come to know later, he is tireless when it comes to things he feels passionate about. He returned on the 13th of February, bearing flowers and a card for me. Valentine's was the following day. The Goose had been running around like a puppy all day, and my wonderful new love was with me. Things were as close to perfect as I had ever known. The next day I'd spend the first Valentine's Day in countless years with a man I loved.

On Valentine's Day we drove along Highway One, the beach ever on our right, and stopped midday for lunch in Pescadero. After lunch we took The Goose to a nearby creek. The embankment from

251

the parking area to the water was steep; Walt and I stayed up top, but The Goose ran up and down with a huge, waterlogged tree branch in her mouth. She'd run up with it, pretend to refuse to allow us to take it from her, and eventually give it up so Walt or I could toss it back into the creek. Then she would burst down the cliff, recapture it, and return it to the top for us to throw again. She'd been on the pills for four days and doing great.

When we were finally able to coax The Goose back into the car, we continued on to Bonny Doon Winery just south of Pescadero, and while The Goose caught her breath in the car, we enjoyed our first Valentine's Day. The winery poured fine wines offered up with rich chocolates, and they even had a poetry contest, which I promptly joined. Walt said my poem should win, but it did not. I didn't care as long as I was a winner with him. We returned to Annie's house that evening and had a simple dinner. Later, when I fed The Goose, it concerned me that she would not eat; she seemed very tired, but I assumed it was all of the running and playing she had done during the day. We relaxed, played with Lucy and Joe, and eventually went to bed.

I got up about two in the morning to pee and found Goose in the bathroom, lying against the glass shower door. I turned on the light to check her out and saw immediately that something was very, very wrong. Hot and jaundiced; her eyes, ears, and mouth were orange. I held cold compresses to her face and sat with her for an hour; until she seemed calmer and cooler. There's no emergency veterinary clinic on the Coast, and it was three in the morning, so I went back to bed (although I did not sleep) for a couple of hours.

Up again at five, I found The Goose even weaker and more jaundiced. Walt was wonderful; he carried my sweet puppy up all those stairs to the van, and we headed up and over Highway 92, out of Half Moon Bay and into San Mateo. Walt carried my precious friend into the emergency room where the vet said there was something unknown attacking her red blood cells, and they could do nothing to stop it. The vet said a transfusion was out of the question because whatever was destroying The Goose's cells would just attack the new red blood cells.

The Goose made it through the night, and after speaking to her vet in Half Moon Bay, we took her back to the Coast. I had no reason to hope, but nonetheless I did. I hoped The Goose's vet could do something. Someone had to do something. They tried this and that, but nothing made sense to me; it was all too crazy; she had only been sore; why the hell hadn't I just used the damned Tylenol? What the hell had I done?

Annie would be home the next day and I'd been scheduled to start the caregiver job in Pescadero later that same evening. I called Billi and explained what was going on with The Goose (Billi knew how much I loved my Goose), and she said to wait another day to start in Pescadero. We agreed that I could come over Tuesday night.

Walt and I had moved The Goose from the emergency clinic in San Mateo back to Half Moon Bay in my van early that morning, so I drove Walt back to Annie's house to get his car, and he returned to Sunnyvale to go to his office for a while. We agreed that I'd spend the night at his house after I cleaned up Annie's place in preparation for her return later in the day.

Mid-afternoon, I stopped at the vet's to check on The Goose. The vet had one idea, something to do with Oxygloben, and I told her to try it. I repeatedly kissed my dear friend and promised I'd see her in the morning. That night was tough. I don't know what I'd have done without Walt's love and support. I slept fitfully and phoned the clinic a little before eight the next morning, hoping for good news.

A vet assistant, who had just walked in the door, asked me to hold on while she went to check on The Goose. I held my breath, each second I waited felt like an eternity. My heart soared when the young lady returned at last to the quiet phone and reported that The Goose was alive and awake. I asked her to have the doctor call me as soon as she came in, and hung up to get dressed and start my day, thinking I'd head to the Coast in an hour or so to see my baby.

I had twenty minutes of happiness before the vet called. She had just arrived at the clinic and found The Goose having violent convulsions. She had sedated her, but she said The Goose was too weak to survive another round of convulsions. The doctor suggested that I get there quick. I don't remember what I said to Walt, and I don't remember driving from Sunnyvale to Half Moon Bay.

All I remember is taking my precious one's wet and limp face in both my hands and laying it on my lap. She was in an oversized cage on the floor. I opened the cage door and crawled in as far as I could to reach her on the bed she laid lifelessly on. She did not lift her head or even an eyelid. I thought she might already be dead, but the vet said she was just heavily sedated. I moved in as close as I could and I talked to her. We had enjoyed many lengthy conversations and I knew this would be our last. I told her how she had changed my life and thanked her for teaching me how to love; I thanked her for the time she had given me, and all the laughter she always brought to me, even on my darkest days.

I asked her to forgive me for my bad decision, regarding her medication. It was my job to protect her and I had failed. I told her she'd always be with me because I'd love her forever. I held her and told her how precious she was for ten minutes, and my heart filled with joy when she opened her weary eyes and looked at me. As usual, as was her way, her eyes said to me,

"Don't worry Momma, everything is going to be okay; please don't be sad."

My happiness was always more important to her than it ever had been to any other being I had ever known. I didn't want her to worry, so I dried my tears, put a smile on my face, and said,

"Oh my silly, silly, wonderful Goose."

We smiled at each other for a minute more, and then her body started to quake and convulse in my arms. I could see the devastation each wave of convulsion brought to her beautiful body. I screamed for the vet,

"Now! Give her the shot now; end this for her, please!"

The vet pushed me aside and administered the lethal shot. Then there was peace; the convulsions stopped, and my Goose laid still, her lovely white furry hair spread out like a sleeping gown. I stayed a while and wiped the drool from her pretty face, and then I lovingly laid her head back down on her final bed and walked away.

Once in the car, the flood came, the sorrow so deep that I had no power to rise above it, so I let it take me down and down into its depths, until certain that I'd never rise again to see the sun. But once the tears were spent and the gagging sobs subsided, I remembered the joy and the laughter, and not just the loss. I started the van and set course for the safest port I ever could have imagined, I went home to Walt.

Letting Go

I wrote the following and ran it in the *Half Moon Bay Review* on February 25, 2004, along with two photographs. One photo was of The Goose sprawled on a rug, and the other was of her in her van with her head hanging out the side window, as it always did. She had more friends that I have ever had.

The Goose
04/23/94 - 02/16/04
Teacher and Friend

She was a common sight around town, her head lolling lazily out of the parked van window, waiting for one of her many admirers to come by and visit. You know who you are, and she loved you all.

She taught us love: She couldn't care less if you were a bank president or a homeless panhandler. Her love was without limits. She had more than enough for everyone and gave it unconditionally.

She taught us optimism: She chased a million birds in her life and never caught one, but she chased the last one with the same joyous abandon as she had chased the first. No bird, gopher, or skunk was safe when she walked the earth. I wish I could say she never caught a skunk either, but sometimes she was a stinker.

She taught us to play: Beach, creek, or roadside mud hole, she was there romping with delight, and later she'd get her jollies by shaking off the water on me or an innocent by-stander. She never cared for the manageable sticks I chose for us to play with; instead, she'd find a huge, water-soaked log and drag it along with us, all the while insisting I throw it for her as I explained, "I can't even pick it up, you silly goose."

She taught us to care for one another: She got me out of bed when I was sad and made me play. She washed my face and hands in the morning, and if I resisted she'd pin my arm down under her paw and continue her work. She reminded us of our worth, delighted in our presence and the company of her many friends.

She taught us: Adventure, joy, silliness, open mindedness, and equality. She lived in the moment and lived each moment fully.

I am a better woman, human, and friend because I had the gift of walking by her side for nine glorious years. She will be missed. Thanks, Goose, for taking time to hang with us mere mortals.

Toni

The Goose was cremated, and her ashes given to the sea off Mavericks Beach in El Granada.

ATG- After The Goose

Billi understood when I called her on Tuesday and begged for one more day. I felt like being at work would help me with my grief, but I needed one night just to cry it out; I didn't want to dump my pain on the poor man I was supposed to be comforting. We agreed I'd be there at noon the following day.

I made the phone calls to the half dozen people who loved The Goose the most and arranged for her body to be cremated. Walt treated me like someone beloved that night. Had I not felt such pain, his love would have filled me with joy. I could not believe my good fortune that he was in my life at this time. I could not imagine walking alone through the loss of my darling Goose.

At noon the next day, I pulled into the long driveway that led up to the modest house that sat on a horse ranch in Pescadero, where the special man I had come to care for had lived his long life. This gentleman turned out to be a well-loved living part of local history, his ranch and his home told many stories, and I found myself enthralled by the beauty that surrounded me. Two very happy ranch dogs greeted me when I stepped out of the van, and I allowed myself to be loved by them for a few minutes, grateful for their energy. I told them about The Goose, and they understood and kissed me all the more.

I eventually made it to the house where I met Robert. Although obviously very ill and weak, I could see the strength and character that made him the living legend that his friends and family so eagerly told me he was. I immediately liked him and his granddaughter. I spent the day just being with him, comforting and cleaning his weathered and wrinkled face that told of joys and tears of all the passing years. Later in the evening I encouraged his granddaughter and her boyfriend to go into town to Duarte's Restaurant, always a favorite of mine, and have a nice dinner. After they left, I sat quietly with Robert and knew that comfort works two ways. As I comforted him, I felt comforted as well.

The granddaughter and her friend returned an hour later with a bowl of Duarte's fabulous green chili soup for me, and the hospice nurse arrived at almost the same moment. Hearing them enter I left Robert breathing softly in his slumber. As I thanked the granddaughter for the soup, the nurse went in to check on her patient. She immediately returned to the kitchen and asked the granddaughter to come with her. Robert had left us. He had slipped quietly away while there was laughter and warm soup in his house. I stayed for several hours as family came and arrangements were made to remove his body from his home.

Late that night I drove the winding country roads through redwood trees that appeared to be reaching for the stars through wafts of transit fog that allowed the moon to play hide and seek with me as I traveled on the abandoned, lonely road. I drove up high enough above the coast to crest the mountain where the state parks sprawl. Night birds startled me out of my deep thoughts of life and death and on and on.

I thought, at this altitude I might have reception on my cell phone. I'd had none down below. I fumbled through my bag, careful not to end up wrapped around a redwood tree, found my cell phone, and called Walt's number. He had not expected to see me for at least two days, and I was afraid he might be asleep, but he answered. I asked what he was up to, he said reading. I told him about Robert's journey that I had for some reason unknown to me obviously been meant to share. Walt said,

"Come over."

I said, "I'm on my way."

I'd been prepared to check into a motel; I would not have asked at midnight if I could come to his home, to his arms, to the comfort he seemed to give to me without any effort on his part to do so. I'd have understood if he'd been in need of some time alone, but I was happy he wanted me there with him because I needed him.

The next morning, I felt drained, completely empty after losing The Goose and leaving Annie's house for the Pescadero caregiver job, only to have that position last a few hours instead of the anticipated weeks or months. I must have been in shock. The mind and heart can only take so much change at a time.

Alone in Walt's home after he left for his office, it all hit me at once. My mind screamed, 'What the hell's going on?' I felt so powerless; I thought, 'What should I do now?'

Walt must be terribly overwhelmed by all this. He must be thinking, Toni Pacini is one screwed up lady; what have I gotten myself into?'

On top of all this self-doubt and complete uncertainty, I also itched. Yes, itched, especially my forearms. I had a rapidly spreading rash. I'd been too busy to think about it the last couple of days, but now that I had slowed down, I had to accept it. I had poison oak. Annie had warned me that her dog Lucy loved to run through the poison oak at the open space area the dog walker took her to daily, and clearly Lucy had brought it home to share with me. Before Walt left for work, he'd suggested I rest for the day; he had pointed out that I had a right to feel kind of blue.

As the morning passed and the itching increased, so did the other symptoms. It wasn't just sadness, fatigue, and poison oak, but lucky me, I also had one hell of a cold coming on fast. Unbelievable! This ought to finish it with Walt. He had already seen me red-eyed, hysterical, basically homeless, depressed, and unemployed. Now the festering sores oozing poison, the snotty nose, sneezing and hacking should finish the job. I felt sure that he'd toss me out in short order, and I couldn't blame him. What could he possibly see in a train wreck like me?

Too tired to even try to call about work or rooms for rent, I went to bed. When Walt came home that afternoon, I tried to pretend I felt better than I actually did. The night passed without any new disaster. The next morning, with renewed determination, I got up, dressed, and told Walt I was going to the doctor. I had to get some medicine for the rash and the cold. I didn't have an appointment, so I spent the whole morning waiting in emergency before I saw a doctor, and after another wait that seemed like hours at the pharmacy, I returned to Walt's house feeling worse than when I'd left.

When Walt came home for lunch and walked in his front door I totally lost it on him. I sat crumbled in a pathetic heap on one of the dining room chairs with my weary head resting on the cool wood of the table. I wept like the beaten and weary soul I was, and when Walt tried to comfort me, I gave him a back door. I felt I had this wonderful man up against a wall. I knew I loved him and he might actually love me at the moment, but I couldn't put him through all the crap that was my life, and it just never seemed to stop, so I said through tears and snot,

"Don't worry, Walt, I'll be better in a couple of days, and I'll rent the first room I find and get out of here. I know I look like hell, and you have every right to be fed up with the chaos and crisis that I cannot seem to stop drawing to me. I'll sleep in the spare room; I don't expect you to be attracted to me, not when I look like this, and I don't want you to get sick."

I ranted on in this fashion for at least ten minutes, and Walt listened patiently. I couldn't tell from the look on his face if he was angry, disgusted, or just plain bored with my bullshit. I always ramble when I'm scared or nervous, as if I can postpone the inevitable pain if I talk long enough. I finally ran out of words to offer Walt to try and tell him how sorry I was for having darkened his door. I quieted and gave him permission to tell me to go away. Empty and ready for the truth, I stilled my tongue, and braced myself for another great loss.

Walt reached for me and took my hand. I rose from my chair as he pulled me toward him and gently guided me into his lap. He said everything I wanted to hear and had not even allowed my heart to hope for.

"Move in here, now. It may be early in our relationship, but you can always move out later if it doesn't work. Stop beating yourself up; stop running, just stop. Rest and heal. Nothing that has happened is your fault, not The Goose's death or Robert's, not the poison oak or the snotty nose. You have every reason to feel sad, so stop trying to pretend you're not, and you will sleep with me. I'm not afraid of a little poison oak, and I never get sick. Now hush and let's have some lunch."

For the first time since I had hooked the jeep to the tow bar on the back of the van and headed South almost ten months before, I felt safe and at home, no, for the first time in my life. I still felt like crap, but I felt like crap in the arms of a man who had shown me that he wanted me, even when I was sad, sick, homeless, broke, and scared. He really wanted me, and I had no doubt now that I would love him fiercely for the rest of my life.

Chapter Twenty - Spitting out the Soap

A day with Walt

Walt's reaching for me. I love it when he reaches for me. We are slowly waking. The day is sneaking past our blinds and sage-green linen drapes. The light of the day is insinuating itself into our cheerful bedroom. Walt wasn't completely comfortable with my need for green when I first started transforming his white and cream-colored sleep area into a colorful summer forest. Walt is monastic. Before I moved in, his home was simple, uncomplicated and white. Don't get me wrong. He has great taste in art, and he had all the usual comforts, but he is not one for too much color. He can live with mini-blinds and skip the whole drape thing, and I doubt that he has ever bought or picked flowers for his kitchen table just because they were pretty.

I felt concerned that I'd overwhelm him in the beginning of our love, but he was great about the little, almost-daily changes, rugs in his bathroom, drapes first in the bedroom, then the living room, and eventually they spread like kudzu to every window orifice in our home. An assortment of other touches of color and items of complete uselessness appeared, like a two-part magnetic hummingbird. One-half of the little bird attaches on the outside of a window and the other on the inside, thanks to the magic of a strong magnet. This gives the hummingbird the appearance of actually being halfway through the window.

Walt came home one day and found the butt of the hummingbird in his face, protruding from the windowpane on our front door. He teases me a lot, but on the occasion that I take him seriously and say I will take down or undo this or that, he always laughs and says, "Darling, I'm kidding. It's just fine. I like it, really; leave it as it is."

I know now when he's kidding, but sometimes I pretend I think he might actually be displeased with me just so I can hear him say, "Darling, I'm kidding. It's just fine."

Whereupon I pretend to be angry with him for teasing me, and usually our jest turns into a wrestling match with me getting the worst of it because I'm ticklish and he is not.

In our sleep we pull away from one another, but as we wake, we slowly start to seek each other out. It usually starts with just a toe. For me it's like testing the water to see if the temperature is tolerable, except I am checking to see if I am dreaming. Is he really there? If he is not, if it were just a dream, then I do not want to wake.

I slowly slide my foot across the wide expanse of our roomy bed and there he is! Day after day I am so delighted to find him there. Sometimes, like today, I awake to feel his toe tickling mine or his long arm twining around my waist and I sigh. I never knew life could be so good, full of love, safe. Now he pulls me to him, and I go gladly. We hold one another in silence for a long time. I have never known such a gentle and caring man. There is no rush, no need for words.

At length I say, "Good morning my love," and he squeezes me in response. One of us will get up soon and go down to pour our morning coffee. Thanks to our automatic coffee maker, we can smell its rich aroma wafting up the stairs, bidding us fair morning. Walt has an early meeting, so he rises first. I linger a little longer in the warmth of our safe nest until the smell of coffee finally gets to me, and down I go to find Walt sipping his and already online checking the day's financial news. I look over his shoulder, but as usual, the stock market is all gibberish to me.

Walt leaves for the office while I'm feeding our wonderful new dog, Camille, and a huge tomcat that recently adopted us, who we respectfully call Albert. We sneak a kiss, but if I stop to chat while Camille's breakfast is on the counter half prepared, she will have a nervous breakdown. Being an abused rescue from the pound, she's a lot like me – she did without for so long that although she now has all her needs met, plus some – she still gets frightened that it may all go away.

The rest of the day flows gently by, and soon I am setting the table for dinner. Walt will be home in an hour. He is always on time and this fascinates me, as I am not accustomed to reliable people in my life. Even more amazing is the fact that he prefers to spend time with me, more so than with any other person or place, and I am honored and overjoyed by this awareness.

I have artichokes ready to boil, and the barbecue grills heating up to cook the ribs I marinated earlier today. Now, five thirty in the afternoon, ribs grilling, chokes boiling, the sweet earthy aroma of rosemary and basil fills our kitchen, and my heart starts to quicken as it does every time I know that I will soon see Walt walk through the door.

Camille has taken up her post, her head resting on the living room windowsill where she watches for his car to pull into the driveway. Albert is curled up in his little bed on the bench outside under the window that Camille is keeping watch through. We are all anxious for his return. We are a pack, and when one of us is missing, although we still enjoy our den and play in the day's sunshine, we are not complete until we are once again all present and accounted for.

Camille's tail starts to twirl in circles; she looks joyfully at me as if to say, "He's here. He's really here."

A moment later the door opens – letting in the hummingbird – and Walt enters weighted down by two bulging briefcases. As he lowers his load to the floor, Camille demands first attention, but she is so excited that she will not be still long enough for him to really love her. He eventually gives up and crosses the room to my waiting arms and takes me in a firm embrace.

The night will be like so many others, now almost a habit, but never a bore. Walt will pour us a glass of wine and we will tell each other about our day. Later in our bed and as the night reaches toward a new day, we will roll apart to rest, only to find ourselves seeking each other with need and love the following morning. Life tastes sweet with Walt. I no longer even taste the bitterness of all the soap I swallowed throughout the lonely years.

Walt promised me that life with him would never be boring, and he told the truth. What he didn't tell me is how sweet it would be, but I wouldn't have believed him. I never realized life could be so good. I had to see it for myself.

Don't even try to tell me that dreams don't come true. I discovered that I was Senior-Cinderella at 49-years old. I'm living a dream that just keeps getting better. Sometimes I find it hard to remember all those hopeless, sad, and frightening years that made up my life before I met Walt. It's like a song I heard a long time ago; I remember it, but in vague little pieces.

On page twelve of this book I shared a poem that I remembered from my childhood. It described the hopelessness my life was and seemed destined to always be, and so I used its words to help you, the reader, understand.

I rewrote that poem the other day in preparation for the conclusion of Alabama Blue. Sometimes you just have to do a rewrite, and believe me, you can choose to do one at any time.

Tiny Tim

I had a little teddy bear – his name was Tiny Tim.
I put him in the bathtub – to teach him how to swim.
First he ate the washcloth – and then he ate the soap.
I called for the doctor – but he said there was no hope.
There was no way I would accept that.
I wouldn't let Tim die!
So I shook him up and squeezed him hard
and watched the bubbles fly.
And as the last one burst and fell as water to the floor.
I laughed and danced with Tiny Tim
and showed the doctor to the door.

"Snake-eyes."

ABOUT THE AUTHOR

Toni K. Pacini

Southern Gothic Author
Poet and Storyteller

Toni is the founder and president of Sin City Writer's Group in Las Vegas. Also a member, ex-treasurer and conference coordinator, in Henderson Writer's Group, the hosts of the Las Vegas Writer's Conference and member of College of Southern Nevada Creative Writing Club.

Published in "Who Are Our Friends" an anthology by Southbay Writer's, Sunnyvale, CA. 2007 and Writer's Bloc IV, an anthology compiled by Henderson Writer's Group. Also Bella Online Reviews – Mused Magazine Spring & Summer issues, 2013.

College of Southern Nevada/Las Vegas' Stylus Magazine 2015, Neon Dreams

Magazine 2015 and Red Rock Review 2015.

Toni returned to college at sixty-years old, she's attending the College of Southern Nevada, Las Vegas, where she's pursuing her Creative Writing degree.

Toni and Walt have been together over twelve years. They live in Las Vegas, with their dog Camille and a yellow tiger-tabby named Suzie Q.

Toni writes short suspense thrillers, poetry, and is currently writing her second memoir, Senior Cinderella, about falling in love after fifty.

Alabama Blue

Made in the USA
Charleston, SC
24 January 2017